How to

Buy a House

Vital real estate strategy

for the first-time home buyer

YVONNE AILEEN

How to Buy a House

Vital real estate strategy for the

first-time home buyer

800 Muses Publishing

© Copyright Yvonne Aileen, 2021

All rights reserved.

ISBN 978-1-7369105-0-4

HOW TO BUY A HOUSE

1: THE DREAM OF HOME OWNERSHIP

It was a summer day in 1982 and friends Rowdy and Angela were spending the night in the Bank of America parking lot in south Colorado Springs, Colorado. They arrived right after work with their sleeping bags and lawn chairs and joined a line of people already there, waiting for the bank to open its doors again at 9 a.m.

The prize for the first 100 customers? A mortgage loan with an interest rate of 15%. The going rate at that time was 2-3% higher, and if Rowdy and Angela hadn't been one of the lucky 100 (they were), they were prepared to pay 18% interest on a loan to purchase their first home.

Homeownership is the dream of many Americans. Beyond the stake-your-claim pride and the stability that owning one's own home provides, real estate is a wealth builder. Home equity is the single largest form of wealth accumulation for Americans and it's in a class all by itself. Where else can you put 3% down (and sometimes 0!) on an asset and realize appreciation on 100% of its value?

Unfortunately, the dream of home ownership remains just that for many people—a dream. They wait for interest rates to drop again or for the time or the deal to be just right. They wait until they can put 20% down or pay off their student loan. They wait for the stars to line up and manna to fall from the skies. They wait and they watch as others buy homes, increase their equity, and live the dream that once was theirs, but that grows dimmer as time passes. Meanwhile, their rents keep rising, saving becomes harder, and in the race to homeownership, they feel like they're wearing clown shoes.

So, if you're feeling like they are, you're not alone.

Income levels have not kept pace with rising housing prices, making "affordable housing" either a national crisis or a national joke, depending on how you look at it.

The best time to buy a house was yesterday. Second best? Today. Don't get shut out of the best opportunity you have to build wealth. Time is your enemy and it's not going to get any easier than it is right now.

Here's a sobering thought: Can you guess the net worth difference, on average, between a renter and a homeowner?

Would you say it was 2:1 ...? 5:1 ...? 10:1 ...?

Not even close.

Every three years the Federal Reserve publishes a Survey of Consumer Finances. The most recent survey found that the gap in wealth between a homeowner household and a renter household is 40:1.

The game is rigged, and the advantage always goes to the house.

I've been a real estate professional for nearly 20 years, and I've seen the difference home ownership makes in people's lives. If I were rich, I'd buy everyone their own house! Failing that, I want to help as many people as I can by sharing what I know. I believe that anyone who wants their own home and is willing to do the work to educate themselves on the home buying process and take a few simple steps deserves to be a homeowner. Not in five years or 10 years, because waiting is a losing proposition. *Right now.*

What are these simple steps?

Step One: Prepare: Educate yourself, learn some basic terminology and the rules of engagement. Learn the best financing programs ideally suited to first-time home buyers that no one ever bothered telling you about. Programs that eliminate credit barriers, provide down payment assistance, and even help with closing costs.

Step Two: Pursue: Select a lender and begin the hunt for the right property, armed with the knowledge that your financing is already lined up.

Step Three: Purchase: Secure your home, negotiate the best deal, and follow through to closing and keys.

Each of these major steps has plenty of minor steps to take. But they're all doable. You may have not saved much—or anything—for a down payment. You may have less than perfect credit. You may not even know where to start and you may not even believe that it's possible. *It is. You can own a home.* YOU.

What You Can Expect

When we're finished with our time together, you'll not only be at the starting line ready to sprint, but you'll also know the smoothest route to take, the hurdles to clear, and the obstacles to dodge to get you across the finish line in record time. You'll know what to do and when, the language to use and with whom, the resources you'll need and where to find them, and how to protect your interests through the entire process. In the quest for your *just right* home, I'll be your secret weapon, your board of advisors, your mentor, your guide, and your genie in a bottle.

My clients pay me thousands in commissions to have access to the knowledge you're about to have. Other real estate professionals who enroll in my courses only hear about a fraction of these strategies and techniques, because there I approach content from a licensee, not a consumer, viewpoint. But for you, in addition to thoroughly covering the basics you'll need to know to prepare for, locate, and secure the property of your choosing, I'm going to share some nuances of negotiation that I've never shared with anyone outside of my own clients because they give us the competitive edge. Soon that edge—and the keys to your new home--will be yours. I'm excited for you!

About Your "Home Work"

At the end of each chapter, you'll find a "Home Work" section. These activities will lead you through the home buying process, step by step. Come back to them or follow them step by step, right across the welcome mat to your new home.

2: THE LANGUAGE OF REAL ESTATE

When conversing with a real estate agent, For Sale by Owner seller, or a lender, it helps to know the vernacular. In this chapter, we'll go over some commonly used terms in real estate. Most people either have no idea what some of these terms mean, or think they do, but don't. After this chapter you'll be talking like a pro. I'll introduce these terms in alphabetical rather than logical order to make it easier for you to reference. Later, when I use a term that may be unfamiliar to you, I'll provide a quick definition as a reminder.

Adjustable-rate mortgage (ARM): With this type of loan, the interest rate can adjust depending on economic indicators. The rate starts out fixed during an introductory period (one year to 10 years) and is usually lower than what you'd get with a fixed-rate loan. After the introductory period, your interest rate can fluctuate. ARMs have caps that limit the total amount that your interest can change over the course of your loan. ARMs can be helpful when interest rates are high, and you expect them to drop or if you don't intend to be in your home very long and the ARM rate is lower than the fixed rate.

Aged funds: This is a term used by lenders to signify that funds you will be using for a down payment or reserves have been in your account for long enough (usually two months) so that the lender doesn't have to ask where the funds came from. Why does the lender care? Because a recent influx of funds could be a loan, which would impact your debt-to-income ratio. Lenders don't like unexplained funds, even when they're in your favor.

Agent: A real estate agent is a licensee who represents the buyer, seller, or, in the case of legal dual agency, both. Unless I'm currently representing someone, I'm a licensee, not an agent. Although it's common to refer to licensees as "agents," and they are certainly agents of their firm, they are only agents in a transaction when they represent someone.

Agency: This is a special type of relationship that exists between a real estate agent and that agent's client. It requires the agent to act in the client's best interests, to disclose any conflicts of interests, to obey the client's lawful instructions, to keep the client's confidential information, to disclose any material facts relating to the property and known to the agent, to exercise reasonable skill and care, and to be accountable for funds, valuables, and paperwork entrusted to the agent.

Annual percentage rate (APR): This is the interest rate you pay for your loan on an annual basis plus any additional lender fees. APR is usually expressed as a percentage. If you see two interest rates listed when you shop for a loan, the larger number is your APR because it includes fees.

Appraisal: An appraisal is an appraiser's estimate of how much a property is worth. Mortgage lenders will require that you get an appraisal as a condition of funding your loan. The appraisal assures the lender that they aren't loaning you more money than what your home is worth. At the appropriate time during a transaction, your lender will schedule the appraisal using an independent third party.

Addendum: A document attached to a contract. When signed by both parties, it becomes part of and carries the same weight as the original contract.

Amendment: A documented change to an existing contract. It changes terms already agreed to by the parties.

Amortization: The process of paying off the principal of a loan over time, spreading out the payments so that at a given point in time (30 years in the case of a 30-year fixed rate loan) the loan balance is paid off.

Asset: This is anything that you own that has a cash value, such as funds in your checking, savings, or retirement accounts, stocks, bonds, and mutual funds.

Broker: In some states, a broker manages and supervises licensees associated with that broker. In other states (Hawaii and Oregon are two examples), all real estate licensees are referred to as brokers and their managing or supervising broker is called a principal broker (e.g., I am a principal broker in Oregon) or a supervising, designated, or managing broker.

Caveat emptor: In some states, sellers are not required to disclose known defects about the property. It's up to the buyer to investigate, ask questions, and do due diligence.

Closing: Closing is when the loan funds and title to the property is transferred and the new ownership is recorded. Most people think of closing, however, as when they sign the closing papers. This is usually a day or two before you'll have the keys in hand because the documentation must be sent to the lender.

Closing costs: These are settlement costs and fees you pay at closing for items such as the appraisal, loan origination and document preparation, and recording. Plan on closing costs of about 3% – 6% of the total value of your loan. However, many closing costs can be rolled into the loan itself, and often you can ask the seller to assist you with closing costs (*see Seller concessions*).

Closing Disclosure: This is a mandatory document that tells you the final terms of your loan. It includes your interest rate, loan principal and the closing costs. Your lender is required to give you at least three days to review your Closing Disclosure before you finalize your loan.

Collateral: When financing a home, usually the lender holds the title to the home until the mortgage is paid off. The home itself is collateral against the loan. Should the buyer default on the loan, the lender could foreclose on the property and take back the collateral.

Comparative market analysis (also called a competitive market analysis or simply comps): This is an estimate of market value prepared by your real estate agent. You should always get one done before making an offer to help you determine how much to offer.

Conforming loan: A conforming loan is one that meets guidelines set by Fannie Mae and Freddie Mac, government sponsored entities (GSE). This is important because lenders can give better rates to borrowers when the loan is conforming. The biggest guideline of the GSEs is maximum loan amount, which is reset annually. For instance, it was $514,000 in 2020 and rose to $548,250 in 2021.

Conventional loan: This type of mortgage loan is not insured or guaranteed by the government. Instead, the loan is backed by private lenders, and its insurance is paid by the borrower in the form of private mortgage insurance when the down payment is less than 20%.

Cooperating agent: This is the agent who represents the buyer in a transaction. The agent "cooperates" with the seller's agent to bring the transaction to conclusion. Don't let the term "cooperating" confuse you. Although the best agents strive for a win-win transaction, the cooperating agent represents you, the buyer.

Brokerage agreement: This is either a listing agreement between the listing agent and seller or a buyer broker agreement between the buyer and the buyer's agent. Listing agreements are more common than buyer broker agreements, but there are advantages to signing a buyer broker agreement, which we'll discuss later.

Carry our own paper: This is a term used by some mortgage brokerage houses to mean that the mortgage broker will fund the loan as opposed to placing your loan with a lender. This is sometimes an advantage to borrowers because an in-house loan may have more flexible underwriting standards.

Closing: When the property changes hands; the seller has the proceeds from the sale, and the buyer is now the new owner. Often people will say *"I closed on my house today"* when they mean they signed the closing paperwork. The closing doesn't occur until the loan is funded and has been deposited in the seller's account.

Commission/real estate commission: This is the amount (usually a percentage of the sale price) that compensates the buyer's and seller's agent. It's traditionally paid by the seller to the listing agent, who then splits the amount with the buyer's agent at closing.

Credit score: A credit score is a number between 300-850 that's based on your credit files. It represents an independent assessment of your creditworthiness. The higher your score, the more creditworthy you appear to lenders.

Debt-to-income (DTI) ratio: This is a formula used by lenders to determine borrower qualification. The DTI is calculated by taking your fixed recurring monthly debts divided by your total monthly gross income. Most lenders want to see a DTI of 50% or lower.

Deed: This is the physical document you receive that proves you own your home. You'll receive your deed when you close on your loan. The deed will also be recorded in your county, so the ownership becomes a matter of public record. *"We're released to record"* is the title company's notification (usually to your agent) that all conditions of closing have been met. As a practical matter, the actual recording of your deed occurs a week or so after closing. There are three primary types of deeds: a general warranty deed, a special warranty deed, and a quit claim deed.

Disclosures: In most states, the seller of a property must complete a property disclosure document to notify the buyer of the condition of the property. This is a checklist of items related to the home (furnace, roof, plumbing) and whether they are in good working order or not. While this is a very important document and should be reviewed carefully, it does not take the place of a home inspection.

Discount points: Discount points are an optional closing cost you can pay to buy down your interest rate. One discount point equals 1% of your loan value. The more discount points you buy, the lower your interest rate will be. Think of discount points as prepaid interest. You pay more up front to enjoy savings over the life of the loan. If you have cash on hand and discount points will help you qualify for the monthly payment, they might be a great option. Otherwise, if interest rates are quite low already and cash is an issue, there's no need to buy down your interest rate.

Down payment: This is the amount of funds the buyer brings to closing (as opposed to the amount the lender will be providing when the buyer is obtaining financing). Many people believe that they need to put at least 20% down, but this isn't true. Even conventional loans are available with as little as 3% down and some government-backed loans allow you to buy a home with no down payment.

Dual agent: This is an agent who represents both the buyer and the seller. In some states this is illegal. In all states where it is legal, it requires advance informed written permission from both the buyer and seller before the agent may represent both parties. Don't be misled. Unless you are working under an agency agreement with the seller's agent, that agent represents the seller only. Never disclose confidential information to an agent representing the other party. In a legal, authorized agency or dual agency situation, you can tell your agent anything and the agent is required to keep that confidential unless there is a legal reason it must be disclosed.

Earnest money: This is a deposited amount (1%-2% of the sales price is common) by the buyer once an offer is accepted by the seller. In the offer, the buyer states what amount the buyer intends to place as a deposit and within how many days after mutual acceptance the deposit will be placed. Your earnest money is at risk should you breach your contract with the seller. It is the seller's recompense for taking the home off the market if you don't play fair. If all goes well and the property closes as scheduled, the earnest money is credited toward your down payment, reducing the amount you must put down.

Escrow: This is a neutral depository where earnest money funds are held for the parties. This term is also used for where your lender will hold your reserve funds for property taxes or homeowners insurance.

Exclusively represented by: Don't let this term fool you. It doesn't mean you can't have your own real estate agent from another firm. It merely means that a single broker represents the seller.

FHA loan: A loan insured by the Federal Housing Administration. Allows qualifying lenders to make loans with easier qualifying standards (modest credit scores, higher DTI, lower down payment).

Fixed-rate mortgage: This type of mortgage has the same interest rate throughout the term of the loan. For example, if you buy a home at 5% on a 30-year fixed-rate loan, it means that you'll pay 5% interest on your loan every month for your entire 30-year term. If you expect interest rates to rise, it's wise to get a fixed-rate mortgage loan.

General warranty deed: This type of deed, used to legally transfer real property from one person to another, offers the most protection for the buyer (as compared to a special warranty deed or a quit claim deed) because it guarantees that there are no outstanding claims against the property, and it includes a promise to compensate the new owner if any emerge.

Government sponsored entity: Fannie Mae and Freddie Mac are government-sponsored entities (GSEs) that purchase loans after they're originated to allow lenders to lend out funds to other borrowers; the intent is to encourage low- and middle-income families to become homeowners. Lenders must meet Freddie and Fannie's requirements to be able to resell them their mortgages so that they have the liquidity to make additional loans.

Hazard insurance/homeowner's insurance: This is a lender-required insurance that must be purchased by the buyer when financing and protects the lender's collateral if the property is damaged or destroyed. It is the "I" in the "PITI," which is explained in a moment.

Home inspection: Hiring a home inspector is part of your due diligence in determining whether you want to move forward with the purchase of a property. An inspector will walk around the home and test things like window seals and caulking, moisture intrusion, foundation cracks, roof condition, light switches, and appliances. The inspector will then give you a list of items that should be repaired or replaced.

Insurance binder: If you're picturing a three-ring binder, you're not alone. It simply means you've arranged with an insurer to insure the home. This must be presented at closing.

Interest rate: This is the percentage of principal charged by the lender for the use of its money. It is paid as part of your monthly mortgage payment and continues for the life (term) of the loan.

Jumbo loan: Also known as a jumbo mortgage, this is a type of financing that exceeds the limits set by the Federal Housing Finance Agency (FHFA). Jumbo mortgages come with different underwriting requirements and tax implications. The value of a jumbo mortgage varies by state—and even county. The FHFA sets the conforming loan limit size for different areas on an annual basis, though it changes infrequently.

Lease option: With a lease option to own, a portion of the lease payment goes toward the purchase price. Make sure you review any lease option contract with an attorney before signing.

Lender: The entity who funds the buyer's loan.

Lien: A lien is interest in a property that helps to ensure the payment of a debt. The person or entity that places the lien is referred to as the lienor or lien holder.

Listing agent: This is the seller's agent who places the home on the market and represents the seller in the sale.

Loan application: A document the buyer completes with either the buyer's mortgage broker or the buyer's lender that lists the buyer's financial condition and assets.

Loan Estimate: Several years ago, the government cleaned up its paperwork and replaced the Good Faith Estimate and HUD-1 Closing Statement with more consumer-friendly forms: the Loan Estimate and the Closing Disclosure. The first of these government-mandated documents, the Loan Estimate is just three pages long. It shows you clearly the terms of your loan including expenses, projected monthly mortgage payment, estimated closing costs, and the amount of cash you'll need on hand at closing. This clearly formatted document allows you to compare loan offers more easily from multiple lenders.

Mortgage: This is the lien you voluntarily give against your property as security for the money you borrowed to obtain the property.

Mortgage insurance premium (MIP): This is a type of mortgage insurance that applies to FHA loans. It differs from private mortgage insurance (PMI) in that there's no option to remove it once you reach a certain equity status. To discontinue paying PMI, you must refinance the loan.

Mortgage broker: An independent licensee who represents multiple lending institutions. Mortgage brokers tend to have more loan types available than a traditional bank lender.

Nonconforming loan: This is a loan that doesn't meet the usual criteria for funding. Often, it's because the loan is higher than the conforming loan limit. Or it may be due to a lack of sufficient credit or the type of collateral used.

PITI: This stands for principal (amount of loan balance still owing), interest (on the loan), (property) taxes, and (homeowner's) insurance. These are usually packaged into one monthly payment, which would commonly be referred to as your mortgage payment.

Preapproval/prequalification: I'm listing these here because they are often used interchangeably but they shouldn't be. A preapproval is a document your lender will prepare that indicates how much the lender is willing to lend you on a home loan. With a preapproval, your lender will verify your credit score, income, and assets. A prequalification is based on borrower statements and doesn't involve asset and income verification, which makes them far less reliable. Sellers will want to see a preapproval letter, not simply a prequalification.

Principal: The principal is the amount that you take out in a loan. For example, if you buy a home with a $150,000 loan from your lender, your principal balance is $150,000. Your principal balance shrinks as you make payments on your loan over time.

Private mortgage insurance (PMI): This is a type of insurance that protects your lender when you have less than a 20% down payment. It covers the gap between 20% and what you're putting down. You can request to cancel this insurance when you reach 20% equity in your property.

Property taxes: You'll be required to pay property taxes to your local government. The amount you pay in property taxes depends on your home's value and where you live. Property taxes fund things like police departments, roads, libraries, and community development. Don't forget to factor in property taxes when you shop for a home.

Prorate/prorations: These are credits between the buyer and seller at closing. They ensure that each party is only paying costs for the time that they owned the home. They will show up as debits or credits on each party's closing disclosure. For instance, if a seller prepaid the property taxes for the year, but only half of the year has passed, the buyer would need to credit the seller for 50% of the property taxes at closing. Prorations are calculated by the closing officer.

Quit claim deed: This is a legal instrument used to transfer interest in real property. The person transferring interest is called the grantor, and the person receiving the property is called the grantee. With this document the grantor "quits" any claim to the property. However, it doesn't guarantee a clear title. A title search and title insurance offer more protection.

REALTOR®: A REALTOR® is a member of the National Association of REALTORS® (NAR). The term is pronounced with two syllables: REAL-tor and the correct usage is all caps with a registered trademark. Not all real estate licensees are members of NAR. Those who are agree to abide by its strict Code of Ethics. This doesn't mean that licensees who aren't members of NAR are unethical, and it doesn't mean that all members of NAR are ethical. It signifies that the individual belongs to a professional association.

Recording: This is the process of official filing of ownership records with the county. The deed, for instance, will be retitled in your name so there is a public record of ownership.

Reserves: This is an amount (often expressed in months' worth of payments) that a lender will require a buyer to have on deposit for taxes, insurance, and mortgage interest. It protects the lender from the insurance company or taxing authority from placing a lien against the collateral (the property) in the event the buyer doesn't pay the bill.

Seller concessions: You may decide to ask the seller to pay certain closing costs on your behalf. If you do, you would make this part of your offer. The seller doesn't have to agree, and some loan types set limitations on the percentage of your closing costs sellers can cover. It's also possible to ask for a seller credit if an item comes up during an inspection that you'd like the seller to cover. We'll discuss that later.

Seller financing: Sometimes a seller will offer to "be the bank" for a borrower who might not otherwise qualify for a traditional loan. The borrower makes payments to the seller rather than to a lender. Rates will usually be much higher than those of a traditional lender. Before going this route, you will want to consult an attorney because it's likely that the contract is written to favor the seller.

Seller's agent: This is the listing agent who represents the owner of the house for sale.

Selling agent: Contrary to how it sounds, this usually means the buyer's agent. It means the agent who "sells" the house, but this is not often the same agent who lists the house.

Special warranty deed: With this deed type, the grantor (person granting the deed to another) promises that no claims have been made against the property during the grantor's ownership; however, it makes no claims or guarantees about any time before that. This may also be referred to as a limited warranty deed.

Term: This is the number of years you'll pay on your loan before it's paid off. A mortgage with a 15-year loan term means that you'll make monthly payments on your loan for 15 years before the loan is paid off or matures. If you hear "30-year fixed" this means the loan's interest rate percentage rate is fixed (remains the same) for 30 years, after which the loan is paid off.

Title: This is proof of ownership. Think of your vehicle title. This is the same idea, only it proves you own your home. It includes a physical description of your property, the names of the legal owners, and any liens on the home.

Title company: This is often the company that holds the earnest money deposit. The title company will conduct a title search to validate ownership and may also handle the closing between the parties.

Title insurance: This insurance protects you from outside claims to your property. The title company will provide this insurance (which you pay for in a one-time fee at closing) after conducting a title search to determine whether there is a clean title (meaning no one else appears to have a legal claim to the property).

USDA loan: These loans are low-interest mortgages with zero down payments designed for low-income borrowers with credit that wouldn't qualify them for a conventional loan. USDA loans are only made in rural and suburban locations.

Underwriting: This is the process in which a lender representative (an underwriter) verifies your income, assets, debt, and the subject property to assesses how much risk a lender will assume if the lender grants you a loan.

VA loan: This is a $0-down mortgage option for military personnel and veterans. It's issued by private lenders and partially guaranteed by the U.S. Department of Veterans Affairs (VA).

Home Work

 Go to YouTube and search for explanatory videos on terms that you'd like to learn about further.

3: ARE YOU READY TO BUY?

It may feel to you as though renting is familiar and safe whereas buying a home and holding a mortgage is the scary unknown. In this chapter, let's try to dissolve some of that fear by comparing renting to owning, including the costs, risks, and rewards of both. When you see exactly what each entail, you may decide that in fact there's less risk in homeownership than in renting.

Qualifying

Rent: When you rent a property, your landlord will run a credit check, verify employment, and check with your former landlord for references.

Own: When you apply for a home loan, your lender will run a credit check, and verify employment. Depending on how stringent your landlord is, you may not have any more difficulty qualifying for a home loan than you do for a lease.

When it comes to qualifying, we could give a slight edge to owning simply because there's no landlord to check references. But we'll call it a draw because the qualifying process requires more paperwork and time for financing than it does for a rental application. It's more work, to be sure, but not necessarily more stringent.

Cost of Entry

Rent: When you rent a property, whether it's a house or an apartment, you'll be faced with certain costs: application fee, first and last month's rent, security deposit, credit report, and perhaps a pet deposit. These may total $2,000 or more depending on the property.

Own: When you purchase a property, you have certain upfront costs and fees (inspection, appraisal) plus a down payment. Depending on the type of loan program you choose, your out-of-pocket costs can vary between $0 and $50,000. Yes, zero. We'll get to some of those options later.

The winner here should reasonably go to renting, but you may change your mind when we get into some of your options for financing. But not everyone will qualify for these super low costs of entry (and even no cost of entry) when purchasing, so we'll call this one for renting to be fair.

Monthly Payments

Rent: When you rent a property, you make monthly rental payments to your landlord, you pay for renter's insurance (or you should) to protect your possessions in the event of a fire, flood, or other disaster, and that's about it. You'll likely pay for some utilities as well, cable and internet service, and perhaps the garbage service.

Own: When you own a property you've financed (as opposed to paying cash), you make monthly mortgage payments to the bank, which include principal, interest, property taxes, and homeowner's insurance. You pay for your own utilities, trash pickup, cable, and internet service.

So, which wins, renting or owning? We're going to call this one a tie for now, because there are too many variables involved.

Maintenance Costs

Rent: When you rent, if something goes wrong with your plumbing or heat, or a lock needs fixing, you can call your landlord and have it taken care of without any out-of-pocket costs.

Own: When you own your property, you're responsible for maintaining it. If a pipe breaks, you need to call the plumber and pay for the repair. You're responsible for the upkeep of your lawn, replacing the roof, and fixing the electrical. The costs to maintain a property can be daunting, which is why the home inspection (which we'll cover later) is so important.

Renting for the win here, hands-down.

Stability of Monthly Payments

Rent: When you rent, you generally sign either a month-to-month tenancy agreement or a one-year lease. With proper notice before your tenancy ends, your landlord is free to increase your rent. In some jurisdictions, there's a cap on how much a landlord can increase your rent each lease period, but generally that cap is higher than you'd like and, in most cases, it's basically whatever the market will bear. Landlords like good tenants but they're in the business to make money and they firmly believe that regular rent increases are a way to protect their investment. In Oregon, which has one of the strictest rent control laws in the country, landlords can't raise rental prices above 7% plus the prior year's consumer price index. Let's say the consumer price index is a modest 1.5%. That means in Oregon, landlords can raise a $1,200 monthly rental rate by $102 to $1,302. That's a big monthly jump for most of us and remember that this is a state where landlords are crying foul for placing a cap on increases at all. Many states have no such limits, but in general, landlords are afraid of vacancies, so they'll try to be reasonable. Let's say an average 5% increase per year.

Own: When you own your home, provided you have a fixed rate loan, your monthly payment for principal and interest cannot rise. Now, your payment may change slightly if property taxes increase (remember that property taxes are the T in the PITI that makes up your mortgage payment). But your payment is not subject to the whims of the market or a landlord.

The win goes to owning here.

Risk of Eviction

Rent: Each month you make a rental payment to the property owner. If you don't make your payment on time, you will be charged a late fee, and if you continue to miss payments, you can be evicted, forfeiting your deposits. The process of eviction can take anywhere from a few weeks to a few months.

But let's say you're the model tenant. You make your payments each month on time. Yet when your lease comes up, your landlord has decided to remodel or sell the property and wants you out. Because you have only a leasehold interest and not an ownership interest, you're forced to move.

Own: If you don't make your mortgage payments on time, your lender can foreclose. This is a long, involved process that can take several months to a year, but in the end, you can lose your home. What about the money you put down and the equity built up? Do you lose that too? Not necessarily. Your lender is not allowed to profit from foreclosure. If your home sells for more than you owe plus the costs of the foreclosure sale, the lender must give you the remainder.

But let's say you're a model borrower. You make your payments each month on time. Can your lender take back your property for any reason? No.

The win for risk of eviction belongs in the own column.

Tax Deductions

You know where the win goes here, right? Can you deduct any portion of your rental costs? No. The only exception is if you use a portion of your rental property as a home office, you could deduct similar home office deductions to those you'd qualify for as a homeowner.

On the other hand, when you own a home, your tax deductions include mortgage interest and property tax payments as well as certain other expenses. You can deduct these from your federal taxable income if you itemize. And when it's time to sell your property, may exclude, up to a generous limit, the capital gain (that is, profit) that you realize when you sell your home.

Owning for the win here.

Equity Buildup

Again, no contest. When you pay rent, it's the property owner whose equity is increasing, not yours. Even when housing prices remain stable, the amount of principal you're paying on your loan each month is increasing your equity. It's a forced savings plan.

Increase to Net Worth

As we've already seen, the average net worth of homeowners trumps the average net worth of renters at an astounding 40 to one ratio. Owning for the big win.

So, let's look at the score so far.

When it comes to cost of entry and maintenance costs, we're giving those two wins to renting. We're calling ease of qualifying and monthly payments a draw, and we're giving ownership the wins for stability of monthly payments, lower risk of eviction, tax deductions, equity buildup, and ability to increase your net worth. Does this mean owning is the right decision for you? Only you can decide that.

A Question to Ponder

How much have you paid in rent so far? How much will you pay over the next one, five, or 10 years? Let's look at how rent pencils out.

If your current rent is:

$500: You will have paid $6,000 in rent in one year, $30,000 in five years.

$1,000: You will have paid $12,000 in rent in one year, $60,000 in five years.

$1,200: You will have paid $14,400 in rent in one year, $72,000 in five years.

$1,468: You will have paid $17,616 in rent in one year, $88,080 in five years.

Why did I include that strange number *$1,468?* At the time of publication, 2021, that was the average monthly rent across the U.S. Your area may be higher or lower, and you can do that math based on whatever you're paying in your current rent, remembering that, unlike a fixed mortgage payment, your rental payments are likely to rise each year.

When we look at the rent numbers we just calculated, in five years of paying rent, you could have put between $30,000 and $88,080 toward your own home.

Which Option Allows You to Live for Free?

As a final consideration, which option gives you the possibility of living for *free*? I'm not talking about "one month's free" incentives that some building owners offer to new tenants. I mean essentially free after a few short years.

Depending on your monthly payment and how the housing appreciation stacks up against inflation, owning your home could pencil out as living for free. Let's take an example.

You buy a home for $300,000 and your monthly payment is $1,200. If housing prices appreciate 4% in your first year, your $300,000 home is now worth $312,000, an increase of $12,000. But you've paid out $14,400 in that first year ($1,200 x 12) so living in your own home cost you a whopping $2,400 for the first year, or about $200 per month.

Could you find a rental you'd want to live in for $200 a month? Not likely.

Each year as your home value appreciates while your monthly payment remains the same, the difference between your monthly payment and the equity earned gets smaller and smaller. Eventually you are living essentially for "free" because your home is appreciating more than your monthly payments. You can ask your landlord if you can live for free after a few years, but you're unlikely to get a yes.

Incalculable Intangibles

There are of course plenty of considerations that calculators can't compute, such as the pride that comes from owning one's own home and the feelings of stability and roots that come with it. The ability to own a pet without paying a deposit, having a yard, owning an asset you can add value to through updates and repairs, the opportunity to create a sense of community with your neighbors, these are all benefits to homeownership that renting can't offer.

Before deciding whether to rent or own, however, consider the following:

- How long do you plan on staying in the area?
- How much flexibility do you enjoy?
- Are you prepared for the responsibility of homeownership?

If you'll only be in town a year or two, renting will almost always be your best choice. You likely won't want to spend the time and money necessary to buy a house, only to have to move again and incur the costs of a sale.

On the other hand, if you plan on staying put for a few years, renting could certainly end up being more expensive than buying.

What if the Market Tanks?

This is a question you should consider. Leading up to the market crash of 2007-2008, many borrowers took advantage of looser lending standards. Stated income, no documentation loans and low adjustable-rate mortgages allowed them to buy much more home than they could afford and borrow much more than they were able to repay. Lenders weren't worried about the loans because housing prices were appreciating rapidly. Borrowers were banking on the rising housing prices and figured they could refinance to a fixed rate later. When the crash happened, homeowners who had borrowed over their heads now found themselves facing mortgage payments on a home that wasn't worth the amount of money they'd paid for it. They were also unable to refinance at a lower rate because the value wasn't there. They were what's known as "upside down" in their home. This is the opposite of what we're used to where the home is worth more than we owe. Short sales (selling a home for less than what is owed for it) and foreclosures were rampant.

So, what's the likelihood of history repeating itself? The Federal Reserve has been propping up the housing market and economy with historically low interest rates. The government tightened lending standards as well. No one wants a repeat of the 2007-2008 crisis, and it's unlikely that the government will let it happen again. Unlikely, but not impossible. There is no reward without some risk.

The risk of renting is a known: pouring your rental payments into someone else's equity. The risk of owning is unknown. We'll never eliminate that risk, but there are plenty of ways to minimize it.

How Secure Is Your Employment?

One element that's vital to consider before deciding whether to buy a home is how secure your job is. Not only will this be a factor in qualifying for a loan, it may also determine whether you're able to remain in your home once you purchase it. Although I firmly believe homeownership is for everyone who wants it and is willing to work for it, I'd be remiss in advising you to purchase a home if you don't have secure employment you can count on in the near term and for the foreseeable future.

If you're in an industry where there's high demand for your skills in your local market, even if your current employer isn't doing well, you may feel comfortable stepping into home ownership. On the other hand, if there's a strong possibility you'd have to move to retain employment if your job disappeared, you may want to postpone a home purchase until you're on solid W-2 ground.

Home Work

Determine your goals. How long do you intend to remain in the area? Are you looking for a hedge against inflation? An investment? A place of your own? Privacy? Proximity to employment or interests? Low maintenance? A yard? Knowing the result you want from your home purchase is an important consideration. Next, research monthly housing costs in your area, both rentals and purchases.

4: CALCULATE
WHAT YOU CAN AFFORD

The most important consideration when contemplating a home purchase is affordability. Affordability pertains to both the house and your own ability to pay. Affordability for a house means you're not paying more for the home than it's worth. Affordability for you means you have the income and stability to continue to make your mortgage payments.

Here's an example. Let's say that you believe you can afford $1,100 per month in a house payment because that's what you've been paying in rent. You get into a home where your monthly payments are $1,100 a month. Is that home affordable? It depends. If the foundation and roof need to be replaced, you'd be in trouble. The underlying value must be there to make that home affordable. We'll discuss how to determine how much a home is worth later. For now, let's concentrate on you. What can you *comfortably* afford?

A lender will look at three key items when determining what you will qualify for:

Your debt-to-income ratio (DTI). As we've discussed, this is calculated by taking your fixed recurring monthly debts divided by your total monthly gross income. Most lenders want to see a DTI of 50% or lower.

Your credit score. A qualifying credit score for the best interest rates for a conventional loan is 720, and some lenders will require 740, but don't worry if yours is lower; you'll see that some loans will qualify borrowers at much lower scores—as low as 500 in some instances. And if you don't know your credit score or how to find it, we'll cover that too.

Your employment history. You'll want to be able to show two years in the same industry at relatively the same rate (and increasing income is always nice too).

Here's an example of how your debt-to-income ratio is calculated.

Your gross monthly income is $2,400. Your fixed recurring monthly debts are $400 for a car payment and $100 for credit card payments. Your debt-to-income ratio then is $500 debt to $2,400 income or 21%. Given that your lender will want to see a DTI at 50% or below, you can spend up to 29% of your income for your house. That means that you could afford a housing expense (PITI) of $696 ($2,400 x 29%). There aren't many houses you can get for $696 per month. That $400 car payment is really impacting your ability to afford a house. Let's sell the car and get out from under your car payment, leaving you with just a $100 monthly credit card payment, which is only 4% of your monthly income. Now you have 46% of your monthly income to work with. That's a monthly payment of $1,104. In all but very high value areas, it's likely you could finance a modest home at that amount.

And let's not forget your down payment. Whatever you can place down on a home reduces the overall cost of the home, your monthly payment, and your DTI score.

Note: The FHA loan program, which we'll discuss shortly, has a DTI of 43% and sometimes up to 56.9% with compensating factors. This is a great financing option for many first-time home buyers where credit score, down payment, and debt may all be issues.

How to Lower Your DTI

The quickest way to lower your DTI ratio is to jettison some debt. Paying down or off your debt eliminates a recurring expense and frees up more cash.

You can also lower your DTI ratio by increasing your

income. Ask for more hours or take on a side hustle. To count this as regular income, it will need to be regular and recurring. However, you can always earn some extra funds temporarily to pay down your debt. For increased income to count on the income side of the DTI ratio, most lenders will want to see the increase over a two-year history.

How Interest Rates Impact Affordability

The rate of interest you pay on borrowed funds can significantly impact affordability. This impact is even greater the more you borrow. Let's look at some examples of how the principal and interest portion of your mortgage payment (total owed after your down payment less taxes and insurance) changes based on the interest rate you pay. Interest rates alone should not keep you out of the buying market. They are a factor, however.

If want to keep your principal and interest payment at $800:

At 3%, you can afford a loan of $165,511.

At 3.5%, you can afford a loan of $159,152.

At 4%, you can afford a loan of $149,694.

So, a 1% increase in interest rates (from a 3% to a 4%) results in nearly a 10% loss in buying power. It means you'll need to shop for a loan that's almost $16,000 lower at 4% than you could afford at 3% if you want to keep the same $800 payment. That affordability gap widens as we increase the amount borrowed. For instance, if we raise the principal and interest monthly payment to $1,200, the buying power of a loan at 3% is $265,810 but at a 4% interest rate, it drops to $234,736, a loss of $31,074, or almost 12%.

So, should you wait for rates to drop? Here's the interesting thing. Sales prices and interest rates are inversely proportional. When interest rates are low, sales prices tend to move upward because low interest rates drive buyer demand and more demand results in shorter supply, which drives up prices. When interest rates rise, buyer demand eventually—not right away, but over time—drops off. Lower demand means increased supply, which has downward pricing pressure.

So, the answer to *"Should you wait?"* is no. Get in the game because you can't win a game you're not in. Just make sure that you're comfortable with your mortgage payment and don't worry too much about what the interest rates are doing. If you buy today and they drop next year or the year after that, you can always refinance to a lower rate.

Tax Deductions Improve Your Affordability

When considering what you can afford, consider whether to

factor in tax deductions for interest and property taxes. These can improve your affordability by as much as 35% overall, but there's a catch. You must itemize to take these deductions. The Tax Reform Act of 2017 raised the standard deductions making itemizing less attractive for many people. Decide whether you're better off itemizing or taking the standard deduction before factoring tax deductions into your affordability meter.

Affordability is in the Eye of the Beholder

Just because a lender tells you that you would qualify for a specific loan amount doesn't mean you have to go for the maximum you qualify for. This is called being "house poor" because you have precious little money left over for anything else.

The U.S. Department of Housing and Urban Development (HUD) has determined that those who pay more than 30 percent of their income for housing are cost burdened, meaning they may find it difficult to afford necessities such as food, clothing, transportation, and medical care. HUD defines severely cost-burdened individuals as those paying more than 50 percent of their income on housing.

Comfortable Now, or Comfortable Later?

You do have to be comfortable with your housing payment, but it's also true that you should buy as much house as you can afford. Why? Because (provided you obtain a fixed rate mortgage loan) your income will rise while your house payment stays flat. So, what feels like a stretch now will be easier in one year, easier still in two years, and so on. By buying at your maximum reasonable affordability, you're controlling a more valuable asset and realizing appreciation on a higher value.

Let's take an example of two fictitious buyers, Jane, and Amanda.

Jane is apprehensive about having a large mortgage payment and, although she can afford more, she purchases a house below her ability to pay for $150,000.

Amanda, who has the same income and financial picture as Jane, decides to "go for it" and buys a house worth $220,000.

Both houses appreciate at 4% per year. After five years, Jane and Amanda can each easily afford their house payments, but:

- Jane's house is now worth $182,498 (an increase of $32,498)
- Amanda's house is now worth $267,664 (an increase of $47,664)

As the years go by, Amanda's equity will continue to

outpace Jane's simply because she started with a higher value asset.

The Dave Ramsey Formula

Dave Ramsey is a financial advisor for the masses and is known for being very conservative with debt. He bases his housing affordability formula not on 50% of gross income but on 25% of take-home pay and recommends a 15-year, not a 30-year mortgage. His formula is far stricter than lender qualifying standards, but lenders are in the business to lend money, not protect your comfort level. You will need to determine what monthly payment works for you.

Home Work

Determine your monthly debt-to-income ratio and calculate how much you have left in your DTI for housing. Begin to gather documentation to prove your income (e.g., pay stubs, W-2s, tax returns).

5: CLEAN UP YOUR CREDIT

Clean Up Your Credit

One item that will determine whether you qualify for most loans and at what rate is your credit score. You'll want to do your best to clean up your credit score and reduce your debt before applying for a loan.

But First, Establish an Emergency Fund

Most experts agree that you should establish an emergency fund before saving money for other purposes. If you use all your available funds just to get across the closing finish line, you'll have to rely on credit cards to fix the water heater that burst in the middle of the night ($1,500), repair the leaky faucet ($200), or replace the 30-year-old furnace that went out in the dead of winter ($8,000). And what happens when you're injured and can't work for 90 days?

Establishing an emergency fund will help protect you against life's unpleasant surprises. Just remember that the money is there for emergency use only—not your down payment, moving expenses, new furniture, or closing costs. How much should you have in an emergency fund? Experts recommend three to six months' worth of living expenses. That's fixed expenses, not discretionary expenses. So, if your fixed expenses are $1,500 per month, you'll want to have $4,500 to $9,000 in an emergency fund.

Next, Check Your Credit

Do you know your credit score? It's a good idea to find out before you apply for a loan. Your credit score is a major factor in determining whether you'll be approved for a loan, and at what rate. To determine your credit score, go to AnnualCreditReport.com. You're allowed to get one free credit score per year (as of this writing, due to the pandemic, they were offering them weekly, but this may change). You can request credit scores from the three primary credit reporting bureaus: Equifax (equifax.com), Experian (experian.com) and TransUnion (transunion.com). You'll want to look at your credit reports at all three bureaus to see if there are any discrepancies you can clear up that may be negatively impacting your credit.

Banks use the following FICO scores when you apply for a mortgage:

- FICO® Score 2 (Experian)
- FICO® Score 5 (Equifax)
- FICO® Score 4 (TransUnion)

Each of these credit bureaus use a somewhat different formula than the industry-specific FICO (Fair Isaac Corporation) Score because FICO tailors its scoring model to predict creditworthiness for different purposes. The three factors that make up your creditworthiness remain:

- Payment history
- Credit use (in finance speak, this is called credit utilization and it accounts for 30% of your credit score), credit mix (credit cards vs. mortgage vs. auto loan)
- Age of your accounts.

The factors are weighed slightly differently depending on the purpose of the credit score, but payment history is the biggie. You need to pay your bills on time.

What Score Is Best?

A perfect credit score is 850, something very few of us will ever hit. I've been at 620 and 780 myself and everything in between. Because lenders look at credit score as one way of determining a borrower's creditworthiness, your score can impact the interest rate a lender is willing to offer you. This is not punishment for a poor score; a higher interest rate is the bank's way of protecting itself for assuming what it perceives to be greater risk. Generally, it takes a score of at least 720 to qualify for the best interest rates.

How to Improve Your Credit Score

If find you that your credit score isn't where you'd like it to be, you can take steps to increase your score.

Pay Off Outstanding Debt

Remember that debt-to-income ratio? Well debt also plays a part in your overall credit score. A good way to improve your credit score is to pay on any outstanding debt you owe until it's paid in full. This not only improves your DTI, but it also improves your credit utilization ratio. This is the amount of *available* credit you have. It doesn't improve your credit score to pay off one card and put the balance on others. Think of your overall credit as a pie. The more of that pie you use up, the less available credit you have. To determine your credit utilization, add up the balance on each card and divide by your credit limit. For instance:

Credit Card 1
Credit limit: $5,000
Balance: $1,000

Credit Card 2
Credit limit: $8,000
Balance: $2,500

Between these two cards, there is $13,000 available credit, of which $3,500 is being used. That means the credit usage is 27%.

Pay Your Bills On Time

Lenders are worried they won't be paid back when they loan you money. What gives them peace of mind is seeing that you reliably pay your bills. This includes all bills, not just credit cards, auto loans, or mortgages. Utility bills and cell phone bills are reported as well. Don't be late.

Don't Apply for New Credit

Applying for new credit just to improve your credit usage percentage is a bad idea. When you apply for credit this is called a "hard pull" on your credit. Too many hard pulls negatively affect your credit score because the lender may think you're racking up a bunch of credit card bills to make a run for the hills. In addition, lenders look at the age of your accounts. Don't close any accounts prior to applying for a loan because that will negatively impact the overall age of your accounts. It's fine to pay off your car, however.

No Credit

Some people have never used credit and need to establish it. Two ways to establish a credit history are:

Take out a small personal loan and pay it back.

Apply for a secured credit card (you place a deposit and use the card, paying it off each month until you can qualify for an unsecured card).

Low, Low Credit

You've checked out your score and ... *whoa*. It's worse than you thought. Will a bad credit score prevent you from qualifying for a mortgage? Well, it would have to be pretty bad. Let's look at some options for various credit scores:

Credit score of 500-580: The Federal Housing Administration (FHA) loan is an option. We'll discuss the FHA loan later. FHA will generally make loans up to 96.5% of the cost of a home, meaning you will only need to come up with 3.5% as a down payment. However, for those with scores between 500 and 580, an FHA loan is still possible; it will just require a larger down payment (10% vs. 3.5%).

Credit score below 500: If your credit score is below 500 or you don't otherwise qualify for an FHA loan, you'll need to raise your score. Other loan programs are available, but they all have higher score requirements than FHA. And even if you do qualify for an FHA loan right now, you might want to wait until your score improves. A higher credit score gives you more financing choices and better interest rates. And interest rates make a huge difference over the course of your loan.

Credit Scores Impact Interest Rates and Interest Rates Matter—A Lot

Let's take two buyers, Juan, and Hector. Juan's credit score qualifies him for the best interest rate at the time of his loan application—4.5%. Hector's had some credit hits and he still qualifies for a loan but will have to pay a rate that's 1% higher than the one Juan pays. No big deal? Big deal! Let's look at the difference 1% makes for these borrowers.

Let's assume both borrow $300,633, Juan at a rate of 4.5%, and Hector at a rate of 5.5%.

- At 4.5% interest, Juan's principal and interest payment is $1,692 each month.
- At 5.5% interest, Hector's principal and interest payment is $1,858.

So, a 1% difference in interest rate increased Hector's principal and interest payment by 10% ($166). And consider the difference these higher payments will make for Hector over the life of a 30-year-loan.

The moral of the story here, of course is that it pays to make sure you get the best interest rate possible, and to do that, you may need to improve your credit score.

What About Student Loan Debt?

Student loan debt will be included in your debt load when a lender evaluates your DTI. However, as with credit card debt and other debt, your lender will only look at the minimum required payment you must make on your student loan each month. If you have $25,000 in outstanding student loan debt but are only required to pay $150 per month, then only the $150 will be calculated in your DTI ratio. You won't be shut out of homeownership just because you have a student loan. Provided you have reliable income and a reasonable DTI ratio, you could still qualify.

Be sure to check how much interest you're paying and whether your monthly payments are enough to pay off your principal. You don't want to go further into debt and then take on the additional financial responsibility of a home.

Home Work

Research your credit score by visiting AnnualCreditReport.com. Total your fixed monthly expenses (e.g., car payment, credit card minimum payment, student loan payment, but don't add in items such as utilities, food, or retirement savings). It's your fixed monthly payments that will determine your total monthly debt (minus your rent payments). Divide this total by your gross income to determine your debt-to-income ratio *before* housing expenses. Is there a way for you to reduce your debt? Decide not to put anything else on credit until you have your new home.

6: GET HELP WITH YOUR DOWN PAYMENT AND CLOSING COSTS

Let's set the record straight—you *don't* have to have a large down payment available to qualify to buy a house. You certainly don't have to have 20%--very few people do, frankly, especially with a first home. According to a 2019 Nerd Wallet article titled "The 20% Mortgage Down Payment Is Dead," the typical down payment for a first-time home buyer is just 7%. But programs are available that allow you to put as little as 0-3% down. It's also true, though, that the more you have saved, the easier your home purchase will be, because you'll likely need some funds to cover your closing costs (approximately 3-6% of the sales price).

Let's look at some ways to get help with both your down payment *and* your closing costs.

Down Payment Assistance Programs

Down payment assistance is available to first-time homebuyers through grants, loans and other government and nonprofit programs. If you haven't owned a home in your own name for at least the previous three years, you're considered a first-time homebuyer for purposes of qualifying for these programs. You'll also need to meet income and credit history criteria, which vary by program, and some programs will require you to complete a course on the mortgage process and financial management.

The amount of assistance you may be eligible for varies by program. With some programs, you'll be awarded a percentage of the home's sale price; others offer a set dollar amount. When investigating options, you'll need to determine how much you'll qualify for, eligibility requirements of the program, and whether funds will be provided via a grant (meaning you won't have to pay it back) or through a loan. Down payment assistance comes in the forms of:

- Grants
- Forgivable loans (accruing at 0% interest)
- Deferred payment loans (at 0% interest)
- Low interest loans
- Matched savings programs

Grants are obviously the most attractive option because there's no need to repay them.

Second in line would be **forgivable loans** (at 0% interest). These are second mortgages that serve as your down payment. The loan is forgiven provided you stay in your home for a requisite number of years. If you move before the required period is up, you'll have to repay all or a portion of the second mortgage loan.

A **deferred payment loan** (at 0% interest) is a second mortgage with the payment on that mortgage deferred. The second mortgage is large enough to cover your down payment and you don't have to repay the loan until you move, sell, refinance, or pay down your first loan. These loans aren't forgiven, so they will have to be repaid at some point (usually when you sell the home), but they can help you get into a home sooner than you might otherwise.

Low and no- interest loans are offered by some lenders and nonprofit and government organizations. These are second mortgage loans that are junior (or in second place) to your main mortgage loan. You can use the funds from this loan to cover the down payment. These loans must be repaid monthly, just as your first mortgage loan is paid.

Matched savings programs are also known as individual development accounts. You would deposit funds into an account with a bank, nonprofit, or government agency. The funds you place are matched by your deposit. Then you can use the entire amount to cover the cost of your down payment.

Here is a list of down payment assistance programs you can check out. Be sure to connect with local housing nonprofits in your community because they may have additional programs targeted toward local residents.

Chenoa Fund: This is a nationwide down payment assistance program with an affordable housing mission. (It's not available in New York, however.) The program is administered by a federally chartered government entity. The fund provides up to 3.5% down payment assistance, which covers what you'd need for an FHA loan. If you have a FICO score of 620 or higher and a DTI of 45% or lower, this program allows you to get a second mortgage with no interest and no payments. If your income is less than 115% of your area's median income and you make your mortgage payments on time for 36 months, this second mortgage is forgiven. If you make more than that, this second mortgage must be repaid. If you miss a payment or pay late, you're given a second chance, but the clock resets on the 36-month good payment history requirement.

Community Seconds: This is a Fannie Mae approved second mortgage that allows you to use funds available from your state and local government and housing nonprofits to fund your down payment and closing costs. It even allows you to use the funds to complete minor repairs and renovations. You'll want to connect with your local HUD office to find out what's available in your area.

HomeReady and **HomePossible:** These two programs are funded by Fannie Mae and Freddie Mac, respectively, and allow qualified borrowers to place as little as 3% down when purchasing a home.

Timing

If you apply for down payment assistance, it may take longer to close on your home. That's because the assistance program will need to work with your lender to secure the loan and the down payment funds. This can add time to the closing process, depending on how quickly the down payment assistance program acts. Just keep this in mind when you make an offer on a house; you'll want to build in enough time to close.

Qualifying for a Down Payment Assistance Program

Most down payment assistance programs will require you to have a minimum credit score of 620 and income below a certain threshold because these programs are geared toward lower income households. Many programs also have debt-to-income ratio requirements you must meet.

Other Requirements of Down Payment Assistance Programs

The home you're purchasing must be in the area covered by the program.

You must be a first-time homebuyer (remember, this means you can't have owned a home solely in your name in the three years prior to your loan application).

You will likely need to attend a class on homebuying and financial management.

You must agree to live in the home for a specified number of years (anywhere from three to 10 years).

The Bank of Mom and Dad

Let's not ignore one of the most commonly used sources of down payment funds: the Bank of Mom and Dad. If you have relatives who will gift you the funds for your down payment, this is optimal. Your relative must write a letter for your lender stating that the funds are a gift, not a loan. This will prevent the gift from counting against you in your debt-to-income ratio.

Getting Your Closing Costs Paid

When making your offer, it's possible to ask the seller to help with your closing costs. This is known as *seller concessions.* This request is usually made at the time the offer is made and may read something like this:

"Seller to pay $6,000 toward buyer's closing costs."

Why would a seller be willing to do this? In a balanced or buyer's market, a seller may be willing to help just to get the deal. In a seller's market, a seller may only agree to this if it didn't change the amount the seller would receive at closing. In this case, a buyer could offer $6,000 above the asking price, but then take it back by way of seller credits to the buyer. This option is great for the buyer because paying a few thousand more for a home won't impact mortgage payment much, but it may make the difference in being able to close on the house because it can help significantly with closing costs.

Be aware that some programs limit the amount of seller concessions. With an FHA loan, for instance, seller concessions are limited to a maximum of 6% of the sales price. These concessions may be used to cover some or all of a borrower's closing costs but they can't be used toward your down payment on an FHA loan. This is an important consideration because, let's say you offered the seller $5,000 more than the list price and then asked the seller to pay $5,000 toward your closing costs. The seller agrees. Then you learn that your closing costs will only be $4,000. You can't get that extra $1,000 back, so you will have paid more for the home than you should. So before using this strategy to cover your closing costs on an FHA loan, make sure you know what those closing costs will be.

A **HomePath** property is another option for having closing costs paid for you, and there are plenty of other reasons to consider this option. HomePath properties are Fannie Mae-owned homes offered to the public at a discount after the previous owner defaulted on a Fannie Mae related mortgage.

A HomePath Home means low down payments and eligibility for a HomeStyle renovation loan. It also provides closing cost assistance – up to 3% of the home's purchase price if you take the online HomeReady home ownership course and then buy a HomePath home. For instance, if you buy a HomePath home for $300,000, you can get a credit for up to $9,000 in closing costs. See *homepath.com*.

Home Work

Search local housing assistance websites for information on how to apply. Reach out to them via email or phone for specific answers you can't find online. Make sure any mortgage lender you choose to work with is familiar with and can work with the program. Research HomePath homes.

7: HOW TO SAVE FOR A DOWN PAYMENT

Maybe you've investigated the 0 down payment options and decided you don't qualify, or you'd prefer to come up with the down payment on your own. It can be hard to save when your rent keeps going up, not to mention other bills and responsibilities. Saving isn't easy, but let's look at some steps that will help.

Step 1: Set Your Number

Determine the exact dollar amount you'll need for the price range you'll be searching in. You may decide to save 20% of the cost of your home to avoid having to pay private mortgage insurance. There are options around that insurance, so don't think that's the only option. Or maybe your credit score is lower than the 580 threshold for a 3.5% FHA loan, so you decide to save 10% to qualify.

Check out an online mortgage calculator (there's one at bankrate.com, for instance) to get an idea of what price range you should be shopping in and how much down payment you'll need. Once you have that dollar figure in mind, determine how long it will take you to save that amount. If it's longer than two years, you may want to look for ways to reduce your living expenses, increase your income, or both.

Place your down payment funds into a money market savings account. You won't earn a lot of interest, but the interest you do earn will help. By way of an example, let's say you want to buy a home in the $250,000 price range and want to put 20% down. This means you'll need to save $50,000. That number—or any other number you come up with—may seem insurmountable, but let's look at some ways to achieve this.

Step 2: Reduce Your Expenses

Let's look at your monthly outgo and look at ways you can cut back. What are your monthly expenses? In performing this exercise, a friend found that she bought a bottle of wine every other day at $10 per bottle. By eliminating this unnecessary expense, she was able to save $150 per month! Here are other areas where you can save:

- Gym membership: $60/month
- Cable: $150/month
- Clothing: $100/month

- Dining out: $200/month
- Drive-through coffee ($5 per day x 20 days): $100/mo
- Lunch out ($10 per day x 20 days) $200/mo
- Nice vacation: $3,000/year

Just removing the first six expenses would save you $810 per month. That's $9,720 per year. Over two years, that's nearly $20,000, and we haven't even had to sell your plasma yet (kidding, of course). Add the savings from not taking two expensive vacations (have staycations instead) and you saved another $6,000 over those two years. These are just a few ways to save; you can probably think of a lot more if you think about it. What can you live without if it means getting into your home earlier?

Step 3: Temporarily Halt Your Retirement Savings

Saving for retirement is important, and you should do it. However, if it's preventing you from investing in your own home, most financial experts will say that it's fine to *temporarily* halt your retirement savings and instead put the funds toward your down payment. If you're currently saving $200 per month toward retirement, that's another $4,800 over two years you can put toward your house.

Step 4: Increase Your Income

Did your employer give you a bonus? A raise? Did you

inherit some cash? Don't spend it—save it.

Next, consider taking on a side hustle or part-time job. Here are just a few options to get you thinking.

- Become a Lyft or Uber driver.
- Search for online freelance work.
- Tutor online.
- Pet sit.
- Babysit.
- Note: Beware of retail work if you're a shopaholic.

Step 5: Sell Some Stuff

You're going to be moving anyway. Now is a great time to jettison items you don't need: books you've already read, clothing you no longer wear, workout equipment that's gathering dust.

And, about your car. Yes, you love it. But if you're making payments on it or it's beyond your affordability level, consider selling it and either taking public transportation (this is becoming a more common choice) or buying something more affordable.

Financial experts say buyers should spend no more than 10% of their take-home pay on a car loan payment. That's still too much if you're saving for a house. I'll go as far as saying you shouldn't have *any* car payment if you're saving for a house or trying to qualify for a mortgage loan unless you have plenty of income to support it because it hurts your debt-to-income ratio.

Not having a car payment improves your DTI and so increases your ability to save.

I hadn't had a car payment in years and my older car was starting to have mechanical issues. I decided to purchase a late model SUV for a very good price, but it still involved a loan payment of $360 per month. That payment didn't seem like a lot at the time, but in retrospect, it was an unnecessary extravagance. Ten months later, I sold the SUV (luckily, I didn't lose any money) and bought a much less expensive car with a $168 monthly payment, saving me almost $200 per month. It was so inexpensive that I was able to pay it off completely just a few months later.

Step 6: Pay Yourself First

Make savings automatic by directing an amount of discretionary income each paycheck into your down payment fund. Most payroll systems will allow you to set this up automatically. If yours doesn't, work with your bank or credit union to make automatic deposits into a savings account. Don't touch this fund for anything. It's not a slush fund. It's your future.

Home Work

Determine what expenses you can eliminate. Brainstorm side hustles and items you can sell. Look at your auto expense: Does it make sense for you right now? Set up an automatic savings plan.

8: SELECT A LOAN PROGRAM

I hope by now you're convinced that home ownership is not only right for you, but possible. And before we go much further, the programs we're about to discuss are limited to owner-occupied. You can't use an FHA loan, for instance, to buy an investment property (one that you don't plan to live in). That's a form of mortgage fraud and people do get caught.

At this point, you may be wondering if there are any homes out there that you can afford. We'll begin looking for properties soon.

Right now, we'll review some loan programs that are geared toward first-time (or first in a long time) home buyers. We've already touched on a few of these, but now we're going to dig a little deeper and introduce you to some you may not have heard of. Here's the big surprise: most *lenders* won't have heard of some of these either! If their bank doesn't offer it, in their minds, it doesn't exist. This happens all the time: A lender who doesn't know that a program is available could very well tell you that you're not qualified for financing simply because your circumstances don't fit *that lender's* offerings. This is just like going into a clothing store that has all size 8s and you're a size 12 and the store clerk tells you, *"I'm sorry, but you don't qualify to wear clothes."* Does that make any sense at all? Sadly, this happens far too often, delaying the goal of home ownership for far too many people. They're given bad information and take it as the final word. Don't take no from someone who *doesn't* know for an answer.

Soon we're going to talk about how to find a knowledgeable financing professional who specializes in first-time homebuyer loan programs. That will open so many doors for you. Enough preamble. Let's talk loans.

The VA Loan

The VA loan comes first because if you're a qualified veteran, active-duty member of the Armed Forces, or a surviving spouse, you have some great benefits just sitting there waiting for you. (If you're not, you can skip this section.) There are service length and other eligibility requirements, but otherwise, qualifying is super easy. With a VA loan, no down payment is required because the loan is insured on the lender's behalf by the Department of Veterans Affairs. The VA loan has no minimum credit score requirement, but many lenders do set their own minimums.

- **Eligibility:** Active member, veteran, or surviving spouse of the Armed Forces
- **Down payment:** $0

- **Credit score:** Lender dependent, but very lenient
- **DTI ratio:** No requirement from the VA, but the lender will require compensating factors for a DTI above 41%
- **Learn more at:** www.benefits.va.gov

USDA Loans

The USDA loan may be one of the best kept secrets in financing. The program, available through the U.S. Department of Agriculture, was designed to help households of modest means get access to housing and mortgage loans in some of the less densely populated parts of the country. Don't let "agriculture" in the name fool you. This is not simply a farmer's loan. And more than 90% of the country meets the criteria of "rural" or "suburban" and therefore most areas qualify for this program.

There are two types of USDA loans.

USDA Guaranteed Loan

The U.S. Department of Agriculture (USDA) guaranteed loan program operates similar to the VA loan, but it's available to non-veterans as well. The 15- or 30-year fixed rate loan is available through qualified lenders and is guaranteed by the Department of Agriculture. These loans have competitive interest rates compared to conventional loans.

Congress appropriates money to fund the USDA program

each year and the funding cycle mirrors the government's fiscal year: Oct. 1 through Sept. 30. If you apply in October, funding might not be available yet, but you may be issued a conditional commitment subject to the availability of the loan. As the funding period progresses, the USDA loan program may run out of appropriated money for that year. Be aware this can happen and discuss a backup plan with your lender.

When there are more applicants than funds, the USDA will give priority to first-time homebuyers and veterans (but as we discussed, most veterans will opt for a VA loan). Make sure you're working with a USDA-approved lender. They're the only ones who can fund this loan.

- **Eligibility:** Property designated as rural or suburban; applicant may earn up to 115% of the average median income for the area
- **Down payment:** $0
- **Credit score:** 640+ (660 has a better chance of qualifying)
- **DTI ratio:** 41% or lower
- **Learn more at:** usda.gov (type in "usda guaranteed loan" or "approved lender list" into the site's search field).

USDA 502 Direct Loan

The USDA also offers *direct* loans to low and very low-income households (those earning 50 to 80% of the median income for the area) who are without safe and sanitary housing conditions and unable to obtain a loan elsewhere. They must be able to afford the mortgage payment, and this qualification also varies by area. Payment subsidies are available. Loans are for 33 years for low-income households or 38 years for households below 60% of the median income for the area. These longer loan terms can help some individuals qualify and afford the more reasonable monthly mortgage payments.

- **Eligibility:** Low or very low income (it must be no more than 50-80% of the median income for the area); also, applicants must be unable to obtain credit elsewhere, yet have a reasonable credit history
- **Down payment:** $0
- **Credit score:** There's no credit floor for the USDA 502 direct loan; some lenders will have their own criteria.
- **DTI ratio:** 41% or lower
- **Learn more at:** usda.gov (type "USDA 502 direct" into the search field).

FHA Loan

The Federal Housing Administration (FHA) insures loans for qualified lenders to enable them to make loans to borrowers with lower credit scores and lower down payments. An FHA loan requires only 3.5% down. On a $200,000 property, that's just $7,000, and FHA allows that money to be in the form of a gift if you've got a generous relative or friend. The FHA also allows the seller to pay up to 6% of the buyer's closing costs (provided the seller agrees, of course). FHA loans are very common and easy to obtain. You can qualify with a credit score as low as 580 and still put as little as 3.5% down. If your credit score is lower than 580, you may still qualify, but you will need to put at least 10% down.

A couple of considerations with FHA loans: FHA requires a mortgage insurance premium (MIP). This can add around $100 or more to your monthly payment. This insurance protects the FHA from borrower default for insuring the loan. It ensures that funds will still be available for borrowers and the program won't run out of money. This MIP lasts through the duration of your loan. With a conventional lender, when the lender accepts less than 20% down, you'll be required to pay private mortgage insurance, but this can be removed once you reach 20% equity in your home. MIP, on the other hand, can't be removed. The only way to remove it is to refinance into a non-FHA loan.

Note: Some borrowers are afraid of MIP because of its permanent nature. But if paying another $100 a month at a favorable interest rate and favorable terms and a low down payment helps you get into a house, I say hooray for MIP!

One additional benefit of an FHA loan is that it's

assumable. This means that when it's time to sell your home, if the interest rates have risen substantially, you'll have an attractive option for buyers. This may enable you to get more for your home than you would otherwise.

Example:

You purchase a home using an FHA loan for $300,000 at an interest rate of 4%. Six years later, interest rates have risen to 8%. You still owe $250,000 on your home, which is now worth $400,000. A buyer can purchase your home for $400,000, assume your loan of $250,000 at a 4% interest rate and finance or pay cash for the remaining $150,000 at 8% interest. This gives the buyer a blended rate much lower than the prevailing interest rate.

- **Eligibility:** Steady income and proof of employment
- **Down payment:** 3.5% (can be in the form of a gift or grant)
- **Credit score:** 580 for the 3.5% down option; as low as 500 if you can put 10% down. Some FHA-approved lenders may require a higher credit score.
- **DTI ratio:** 43% and sometimes up to 56.9% with compensating factors
- **Learn more at:** fhalenders.com

FHA Good Neighbor Next Door

Are you or your partner a teacher, law enforcement officer, firefighter, or emergency medical technician? If so, you should know about the FHA Good Neighbor Next Door program. This program allows qualified borrowers in one of these professions to buy foreclosed FHA-insured properties in designated revitalization areas at a 50% discount with a down payment of only $100! Yes, you read that right. You purchase the home at a 50% discount. The other 50% you carry as a "silent second" mortgage, for which you make no payments. This silent second disappears after you live on the property for at least three years.

- **Eligibility:** At least one borrower must be employed full time as a law enforcement officer, K-12 teacher, firefighter, or emergency medical technician and the borrower must agree to live on the property for at least 36 months
- **Down payment:** $100
- **Credit score:** 580 (again, some approved FHA lenders may require a higher score)
- **DTI ratio:** May not be applicable due to the 50% discount
- **Learn more at:** hud.gov (search "good neighbor next door")

FHA Rehabilitation Loan

What if you find a property you'd like to make an offer on, but it needs an overhaul? Enter the FHA 203(k) rehabilitation loan. The FHA 203(k) program lets you roll up to $35,000 of repair, improvement, or upgrade costs into your loan. This might include repairs requested by an appraiser or inspector at the time the property is being evaluated for purchase. There are two 203(k) programs:

The 203(k) Streamline loan (also called Limited 203(k)) is for minor repairs of between $5,000 and $35,000 and may be used for kitchen or bathroom updates, energy efficiency improvements, etc. The upper limit of $35,000 in repair costs includes a 15% buffer for cost overruns, so your actual repair costs shouldn't exceed $31,000).

The 203(k) Standard loan allows you to use rehab funds for all repairs except for luxury repairs. This can even include razing the building and starting from scratch (provided the foundation remains), structural alterations, converting a one-family home into a duplex, etc. Projects must be completed within six months.

- **Eligibility:** Steady income and proof of employment
- **Down payment:** 3.5% (can be in the form of a gift or grant)
- **Credit score:** 580 for the 3.5% down option; as low as 500 if you can put 10% down. Note that some approved

FHA lenders may require a higher score.

- **DTI ratio:** 43% and sometimes up to 56.9% with compensating factors
- **Learn more at:** hud.gov (search "fha 203(k) loan")

Conventional Financing Low Down Payment Options

Usually when you hear "conventional loan" you think of a 20% down payment. But conventional loans are available with as little as 3% down, which beats an FHA loan by 0.5%!

Conventional loans are merely loans not backed by a government agency but instead conform to the guidelines established by Fannie Mae and Freddie Mac, making them "conforming loans." More than half of mortgage loans funded in the U.S. are conventional loans.

Underwriting standards are stricter with conventional loans than with governmental loans. And if your down payment is lower than 20%, you'll be required to purchase mortgage insurance, but this is cancellable when one of two events occur.

You've paid down your mortgage balance to 80% of the home's original appraised value. For this option, you must initiate the removal of the mortgage insurance with your lender.

Your loan balance drops below 78% (the mortgage servicer is required to eliminate PMI automatically).

- **Eligibility:** Steady income and proof of employment
- **Down payment:** As little as 3% with PMI

- Credit score: 620 (740 will get you better interest rates).
- DTI ratio: 45%. Exceptions can be made for DTIs as high as 50% with strong compensating factors such as a high credit score and/or lots of cash reserves.
- Learn more: at your favorite lender.

Piggyback Loans

Don't let the cute name fool you; this loan has a lot to offer. One type of a piggyback loan is an 80/10/10 loan (it may also be referred to as a package loan). With this loan, you secure an 80% first mortgage and a 10% second mortgage, placing just 10% down. This option allows you to avoid having to purchase private mortgage insurance. With a piggyback, the 80% part of the loan is usually a 30-year fixed-rate mortgage, and the second 10% mortgage is a shorter-term loan with a somewhat higher interest rate. A condo alternative is a 75/15/10 (interest rates are higher for condominium loans when the first mortgage exceeds 75%).

An advantage of the piggyback loan is that you can pay off the second loan without having to refinance the entire loan, reducing your monthly mortgage payment. Some clients of mine used a piggyback loan to purchase a home before selling their first home. They were in a hot seller's market and were concerned that if their house sold too soon, they'd end up homeless if they were unable to locate a replacement property.

So rather than listing their home for sale first, they instead purchased their replacement home using a package loan, then they paid off the smaller loan when their first house sold.

Eligibility for a piggy back loan is the same as with conventional financing, and you can learn more from conventional lenders and mortgage brokers.

HomeReady and Home Possible Loans

Two options for lower income borrowers and those with lower credit scores are the HomeReady and HomePossible loans. Terms are similar so we'll discuss just the HomeReady loan.

The HomeReady loan is a Fannie Mae loan program and offers a 3% down payment option (which can come from a gift or down payment assistance program). It also allows you to use the income from a non-occupant co-borrower or non-borrowing household member, or rental income from a basement apartment or mother-in-law suite to qualify.

- **Eligibility:** Low income (80% or less than area median income); must participate in a homeownership course; you don't have to be a first-time homebuyer, but you can't currently own a home
- **Down payment:** As little as 3% with PMI and it can be entirely funded with a gift.
- **Credit score:** 580 (alternate credit reporting is allowed, where a solid rental history may be considered)

- **DTI ratio:** 45% and no more than 38% can go toward housing (for those with 620 or higher, DTI can be somewhat higher)
- **Learn more at:** fanniemae.com: search "homeready" and freddiemac.com (search for "homepossible")

Seller Financing

Sometimes, no financing program is available that meets your specific circumstances. In such cases, you may want to approach a seller about financing your purchase. There are two primary ways to use seller financing:

- A land sales contract
- A purchase money mortgage

Land Sales Contract

The land sales contract is known by several other names: land installment contract, contract for deed, or simply land contract. Don't let the name fool you—it's not a vacant land sale. With this type of financing, the seller will finance all or part of your purchase. You make loan payments directly to the seller who retains ownership (but not possession) of the property until you pay off the loan by completing payments through the terms of the loan, or more commonly, by refinancing a few years down the road. You negotiate your terms, interest rates, etc., with the seller. Your closing costs will likely be lower than with traditional financing. However, because the seller is taking on some risk and isn't receiving the proceeds from the sale in a lump sum, interest rates will almost certainly be higher. This type of agreement is filled with landmines and legal advice is vital.

Purchase Money Mortgage

Another type of seller financing is the purchase money mortgage, also called a seller carry back. With this financing, you give a mortgage to the seller toward the sales price, and you keep the title. The reason this option is referred to as a seller carry back is because the seller carries back a portion of the sales price through a second mortgage you assume.

Example

You're unable to qualify for a loan for the entire purchase of the seller's property. So, you take out a loan for 80% of the sales price and your attorney drafts a mortgage for the remaining 20%. This mortgage is recorded, protecting both you and the seller from future misunderstandings.

The differences between the land contract and purchase money mortgage are that a seller receives more money up front with a purchase money mortgage, and you hold the legal title; with a land contract, the seller may receive only a down payment up front but will retain legal title until the balance of the purchase price is paid.

To learn more, seek advice from an attorney before forming a contract with either of these financing programs.

Home Work

Visit the sites mentioned for more information on each loan type. Select one to two programs that may be right for you.

9: SELECT A LENDER
AND GET PREAPPROVED

Now that you've got a good idea of several loan programs, how do find a lender to work with you on one of them? Remember that not every lender will be familiar with or approved to fund all these loans. Before we select a lender, let's start by reviewing the differences between a traditional lender, such as a loan officer at a commercial bank, and a mortgage broker.

Loan Officer vs. a Mortgage Broker

When you visit your local bank or credit union, the loan officer there can only offer you the mortgage options available through that financial institution.

A mortgage broker, on the other hand, can match you with options available through many different lenders. The mortgage broker negotiates on your behalf and because a mortgage broker works with many lenders, he or she can help you find the loan programs with the best rates, terms, and lowest closing costs for your situation.

The mortgage broker originates loans but usually does not fund them (although some do "carry their own paper," meaning the brokerages fund some loans).

A loan officer works for a bank, credit union or mortgage lender and the lender they work for funds the loan; you'll typically make payments to the same lender after closing.

Both professionals review your loan application and financial paperwork to make sure you meet the minimum mortgage requirements.

With a mortgage broker you:
- Get rates and fees from multiple lenders
- Wait for the lender to make the final approval decision
- Get assistance with mortgage shopping
- Have more loan products to choose from
- Can switch lenders if your loan is denied
- Aren't working directly with the entity who will approve your loan or lend you money directly

With a loan officer you:
- May get a break on rates and closing costs, depending on your relationship with the bank
- Have interest rate options limited to those available at that financial institution
- Will have an "in house" approval and receive money

directly from that institution

- Are limited to the loan options offered at that lender
- May get an exception for unique income and financial situations
- Need to start over with a new lender if you're denied.

Both mortgage brokers and loan officers are considered mortgage loan originators (MLOs), and both must meet strict federal requirements to negotiate mortgage loans.

You can research the background of a mortgage loan originator through the Nationwide Multistate Licensing System (NMLS) and the Consumer Financial Protection Bureau (CFPB).

So, which is better, a commercial lender or a mortgage broker? It depends on the loan program you've selected. My personal bias, and what most of my clients have found, is that mortgage brokers offer you more options and better personalized service. Whichever route you go, interview several professionals to determine your comfort level. If you have trouble getting one of them to call you back, how vested are they in helping you?

Finding Your Partner in Financing

Here are some options for finding your lender:

If you know someone who just purchased a home, you might ask for a referral. This option is best if your friend secured the type of loan you're interested in obtaining.

Enter the following in Google search field:

[name of loan program] [approved lender] [city/state]

If you're pursuing a down payment assistance grant, you can contact the local organization who offers these to learn about qualifying.

You can visit the websites already mentioned under "learn more" and search for a list of approved lenders.

You can attend first time home buyer programs in your area (be aware that some of these will be merely sales pitches for a specific program or lender).

You can look at mortgage brokerage web sites in your area and review the bios of the various brokers. Look for one who specializes in first time home buyer loan programs.

Interviewing Lenders

Once you've selected a few lender candidates, interview them. Here are some questions you may want to ask. The most important consideration is whether the lender has experience connecting borrowers with the type of loan you've identified.

- What has been your experience with this type of loan program?
- Is there a better program out there for me?
- What are your typical fees?

Note that when you apply for a loan, you will be given an estimate of all these fees in a document called the Loan Estimate. The Loan Estimate will ask for your name, Social Security Number, address of the property you are making an offer on, the estimated value of the property, the loan amount, and your income. But you can also ask for an estimate of these costs before you apply for the loan.

Ask about a rate lock. We've seen what a difference interest rates can make, and they do change daily, so ask if the lender will charge a fee to lock in a loan rate. If so, ask how much the lock will cost you, if it protects all the loan costs or simply the interest rate, and if you'll be given the lock rate in writing. If you decide not to lock your rate, you'll have to pay whatever the prevailing rates are at the time you apply for your loan.

Ask whether a prepayment penalty applies to the type of loan you're considering. If you pay off your loan before a specified period, some lenders will want to be compensated for the interest they didn't get to charge you (because you paid off your loan early). Charging a prepayment penalty is forbidden in many states, but not in all, so it's a good idea to ask if there is one, for how long the prepayment penalty period applies, and what the fee is. Even if you don't think you'll pay off the loan, you may want to refinance before the prepayment penalty period is over, which would prompt the penalty.

Ask how long it will take to fund the loan you have in mind. This is crucial, because when it's time to make an offer on a home, you'll need to let the seller know when you expect to close, and you don't want to box yourself into a corner. The average loan processing time is approximately 45 days, but some government programs may take longer.

If you have any other questions, ask them! No question is too naïve, and no one expects you to know everything. Answering consumer questions is what finance providers do every day.

Get Preapproved

Getting pre-approved is the first step you should take if you're serious about buying a home. While it may seem intimidating at first, this is your ticket to wealth building, and a home of your own.

Preapproval vs. Prequalification, and Soft Pulls vs. Hard Pulls

Remember that a preapproval is not the same thing as a prequalification. A prequalification is based on a borrower's statements to a willing lender. It is a "soft pull" on your credit. A pre-approval is a "hard pull" and digs deeper. For this reason, you want to have selected your lender or at least be close to pulling the trigger on applying for a loan before getting preapproved. Too many hard pulls on your credit over too long of a period will decrease your credit score!

Here's the scoop:

Hard pulls suggest an intent to borrow (read: increase debt).

They can knock your credit score down between 5 and 20 points depending on which credit bureau is doing the reporting. Soft pulls don't pack the same punch. However, you *can* apply for multiple pre-approvals over a short period of time (two weeks to 45 days depending on the reporting bureau) and these *should* only count as one hard inquiry. Hard inquiries remain on your credit report for two years, so be sure you're ready to buy before you begin asking for preapprovals.

Why get one at all? Because they carry more weight, most sellers will require you to provide a pre-approval letter before considering your offer.

It's a good idea to get prequalified first. If you can't get prequalified, there's no sense in attempting to get preapproved because of the hit your credit score will take.

This is not the end of the world. It's better to know now before you start shopping and get your heart set on a house. And the process will help you understand what you need to do to get your finances in order.

But let's think positive: Let's say you've been preapproved. What does that get you? Nothing less than a ticket to buy! You'll know exactly what you qualify for and the price range you should be shopping in. Consider your preapproval as your maximum. You won't want to shop (or even look) above that number.

Especially in a seller's market, you will need every competitive advantage. Having your pre-approval in place will demonstrate to the seller that you're serious and qualified.

How Long Does It Take?

Preapproval can take several days to a few weeks to complete, depending on your financial situation and the type of loan you're going for (and frankly, how busy the market is). This is why it's so important to put this step ahead of shopping for a new home.

Preapproval Paperwork

If you hate paperwork, this isn't going to be any fun at all. Just keep that dream house in mind as you slog through the bureaucracy. You'll need:

- Pay stubs issued in the last 30-60 days (and if approval drags on, expect to be asked for updated stubs later)
- Two years of W2s or tax returns
- Quarterly account statements for assets
- Two months of bank statements

Home Work

If you haven't already done so, request a copy of your credit report. Review it and fix any errors you find. Determine your budget for a monthly mortgage. Create a short list of lenders and interview them. Can they assist you with the loan program that's best for your situation? Get prequalified (or preapproved if you're close to being ready to buy) to identify the price range in which to shop. Remember that there are two prices here: one that you qualify for and one that you're comfortable paying. Don't go outside of your affordability comfort zone.

10: THE "JUST RIGHT" HOUSE

Goldilocks was a savvy shopper. Not for her the too-cold porridge or the too hard bed or the too fragile chair. She was looking for something that was *just right*. The Goldilocks strategy will serve you well when you search for a home. You're neither looking for a McMansion nor something you dread coming home to. Your *just right* home will meet your goals of homeownership, give you a chance to build equity, and be something you can eventually be proud to show off (even if it requires a little elbow grease to get it there). Set your expectations accordingly. The end goal is home ownership, which gives you financial stability, allows you to increase your net worth, and gets you in the game. Be willing to buy an ugly duckling that you can one day turn into a swan.

Example:

Erin worked at a salon and her income was sporadic. She'd

not been able to save much. Her dad offered to gift her the down payment of 3.5% so she could get an FHA loan. Erin found a two-bedroom, two-bathroom ranch for $300,000. She didn't love the fact that one of the bathrooms was engulfed by a huge, jetted tub separate from the shower, leaving little room for her styling products. However, it was the only home available in her price range and she decided she could one day remove the tub and install a space-saving shower/tub combination.

What Type of Home Do You Want?

To begin shopping, let's consider some basic questions.

What type of home do you want? A condo? A small starter home? A fixer? If you're handy with tools or can paint, you may want to look for a home that needs a little work. Do you need a yard, or would you prefer low maintenance? What are your deal killers, and what are your must-haves? Is location more important to you than the house itself?

Chances are that your price range will dictate both the type of home you can afford and where it's located. Forget about your dream home for now. It will happen eventually, but first comes reality. Your *just right* home will almost certainly be a starter home and you'll have to make some compromises. Don't compromise on your price (stay within your comfort zone), your safety, or your health. Everything else is negotiable.

Besides price, here are the criteria you'll want to consider:

- **Size:** This may matter less than the layout, but you likely have an idea of what's too small for you. You may be surprised, though. I moved to Maui for two years and although I never thought it would be possible, lived very happily with my grown son and two small dogs in a two-bedroom 771 square foot condominium. Layout makes a big difference!

- **Number of bedrooms:** Do you really need three, or will two work if a bonus area is available?

- **Number of bathrooms:** One? One and a half? Two? A full bathroom means it has a shower, tub, or both, plus a toilet and sink. A half bath has a toilet and sink only. Often, one and a half bathrooms will do even if you think you need two, so keep an open mind. And if it's just you, you can likely get by with one. Remember, this is your *just right* house, not your *just right plus* house.

- **Location:** This is an important consideration. However, if you find that all the homes in your preferred location are out of your reach financially, you'll need to expand your search. Look for adjacent neighborhoods (over time these can take on the "glow" from the more desirable neighborhoods nearby) and spread out from there.

- **Property type**: Do you want a condominium, a stand-alone house? A townhouse? A town house, by the way, is usually built on two or more levels and shares one or two walls with adjacent homes but has its own entrance and often its own small yard. Townhouses and condominiums will likely have association dues, which will impact affordability, but may provide features you otherwise would have to pay for (lawn maintenance, for instance).
  - Kitchen size and layout
  - Location of primary bedroom
  - Sun exposure
  - Age of home
  - Condition of home (how much work are you willing to do? Cosmetics? Repairs?)

Here are some typical deal killers clients of mine have had. This doesn't mean they're your deal killers. I list them only to give you something to think about.

- Any property in a flood zone or with drainage issues
- Any property with a homeowners association
- A property for which the insurance is too high because it's in a disaster zone or has had flooding issues

- Any property on "stilts"
- Any property with a flat roof (maintenance issues)
- Property taxes above a given dollar amount
- A property built prior to 1978 (where lead-based paint may be an issue)
- Popcorn ceilings (an easy fix, however)
- A house with fewer than 1.5 bathrooms
- A house with fewer than 3 bedrooms
- A house with more than 4 bedrooms
- A house without a fenced yard
- A house with a garage too small to accommodate the buyer's car
- A house that doesn't have a bathroom on every floor that has a bedroom
- A kitchen without a dishwasher
- Houses next to public spaces, parking lots, churches (the noise of bells every Sunday morning was a concern), shopping centers, etc.
- Houses under major power lines
- Houses on busy streets
- Houses with gravel roads
- Houses in hilly areas, making winter commutes treacherous

- Houses that already had all the cosmetics done so there's no upside potential
- A property with too big of a yard
- Houses with neighbors who have sketchy yards
- Single-story houses
- Multiple-story houses

You get the idea. Try to keep an open mind. If you narrow your criteria too much, you'll restrict your ability to get into a home of your own. If you find that fewer than 10% of the homes in your market that match your criteria are in your price range, you will likely need to expand your geographic area or compromise in some areas.

And don't be surprised if what was a deal killer suddenly doesn't matter so much anymore when you find your *just right* home.

Some buyer clients of mine, a young couple, told me they absolutely did not want to be on a busy street. Therefore, I didn't show them a new listing that had come up in a school district they had in mind for their daughter because it was along a busy street. The couple phoned me at 8:00 one evening and said they'd just seen a house for sale and would like to see it that night. When they gave me the address, I said, *"But that's a busy street."* They said they didn't care, because it happened to back up to the playground of the school their daughter would attend. We were able to tour the house that night and I wrote an offer for them, it was accepted, and they moved in a month later.

There's a saying in real estate that I don't like because it sounds insulting: *"Buyers are liars."* What it means is that often buyers have an idea of what they want (or in this case what they didn't want), but when they see their *just right* home, deal killers and must-haves go right out the window.

Let's look at some likely suspects for your first, *just right* home.

Affordable Home Options

Condominiums: Condominiums are entry level homes and are usually much more affordable than detached homes. But they are still real estate, and you can still build equity! However, before purchasing a condominium, you'll want to review a packet of information the seller will request from the condominium association and provide to you.

Because condominiums share common areas, maintenance costs for siding, roofs, sidewalks, roads, etc., are shared among the owners and are covered by the association dues condominium owners pay each month. Sometimes, to keep those dues low, there may not be enough funds held in reserves when a large expense occurs. A client of mine was looking at some condominiums in downtown Portland on the river. Her friend had purchased a condominium there and the idea of looking out over the Willamette River and living downtown appealed to my client. She ultimately decided against the move and was soon very glad she'd made that call. Her friend received an assessment for $50,000 within six months of purchasing her unit. The siding on all the units had to be replaced and there wasn't enough in the reserve funds to cover the expense. Therefore, all owners were assessed $50,000. This is an extreme example, but it's not rare. Know the risks when purchasing a condominium and look through association board minutes for hints that an assessment may be coming.

Another risk with condominiums is that lenders won't finance a condominium purchase if there's ongoing litigation between the association and a contractor, for instance. This happened to another client. She had inherited a unit from her aunt and wanted to sell it but couldn't until the litigation was settled unless she could find a cash buyer.

Fixers: Don't overlook a home just because its front porch needs to be replaced or it needs new windows; not even if the previous occupant yanked the built-in oven out of the wall. Provided the fixer is financeable (and remember that the FHA

203(k) loan is designed to roll rehab costs into a home loan), you may find a diamond in the rough that just needs a little work to turn into a nice home. Most buyers are looking for move-in ready homes. If you're willing to overlook a few warts, you might pick up a bargain.

HomePath: Remember that HomePath homes are Fannie Mae-owned homes offered to the public at a discount after the previous owner defaulted on a Fannie Mae-owned mortgage. (See homepath.com.) I've helped clients purchase HomePath homes and the inspections have gone well and their closing costs were covered by the program.

Foreclosures: Foreclosure homes are an option for first-time homebuyers, but I don't recommend them. Title issues, a limited ability to inspect before you buy, and serious and often hidden damages caused by angry homeowners (think a bag of concrete flushed down the plumbing, electrical wiring ripped from walls) can mean huge repair expenses. However, Fannie Mae foreclosures (i.e., HomePath) are examples of foreclosed properties that I would consider in your search.

REOs: REOs, as well, are foreclosed properties that are worth considering. They have been taken back by banks after the properties fail to sell at a foreclosure auction (REO stands for *real estate owned*). Banks don't like to have real estate on their books—they're in the business to lend money—and so they often sell these homes for a discount. In addition, they will at least have had an asset manager review the property to determine its likely value and to bring it up to reasonable market readiness. Therefore, I'm more comfortable recommending this category for your home search than some other types of foreclosures.

You can find REO properties by doing a little research. Most lenders compile lists of all their available REO properties (e.g., foreclosures.bankofamerica.com or simply search "[name of bank] foreclosure properties").

HUD Homes: The U.S. Department of Housing and Urban Development (HUD) has homes for sale. The first house I ever bought was a HUD home, and HUD had an ad campaign going at the time that read *"Buy a HUD Home, Quick Before It Falls Down."* It was poking fun at the perception some people had about the condition of a HUD home. In fact, they were usually in very good condition.

When I purchased my HUD home, there was a sealed bid auction, and I attended the bid opening. I was likely the only owner-occupied purchaser there; the rest were investors who were trying to snap up a home for a bargain. I was thrilled when my bid won but miffed that I'd overpaid by $2,000 because that's how much I overbid the next highest bidder. In retrospect, it was an awesome deal. See hud.gov and search for homes for sale.

Manufactured Homes: *Manufactured home* is the new term for mobile home, a term that fell out of general usage in 1976. Manufactured homes aren't mobile anymore. They're prefabricated units. If you see an "IN-PARK" listing on a multiple listing service, this is a manufactured home in a mobile home park. While "in park" sounds lovely and you might picture rolling meadows and walking trails, this is not a category of an affordable home I can recommend. For one thing, these homes don't hold their value. For another, the rent on the lot can go up steeply, beyond the homeowner's ability to pay and leaving only two options: find $20,000 to move the home or abandon it. And financing is an issue.

Modular Homes: Modular homes, on the other hand, are homes built offsite and moved to a location. Because they're factory built, they are tightly constructed and strong; unlike manufactured homes, they can even be built as two-story structures.

Tiny Homes: Tiny homes are generally defined as those with less than 600 square feet. They may be built on a foundation or on a trailer. Some jurisdictions don't allow them to be built on land and sold as real property; they may be considered personal property. This isn't the best avenue for affordability or financing.

Stale Bargains: I've seen this happen, and it's sad—except for the lucky buyer. A seller will list a home at too high of a price. Sometimes this happens because a listing agent fails to be straight with the seller about the home's true market value and agrees to accept the listing at a too-high price. This is unethical, and it does the seller a terrible disservice because a home that lingers on the market becomes stigmatized in buyers' eyes. They wonder, *"What's wrong with it?"* And even when the price begins to drop, this doesn't help. It only feeds speculation about what form of cooties this home is infected with.

Looking for a home that has lingered on the market a while can be an excellent opportunity to pick up a bargain. Think about it from the seller's standpoint. They list their home for sale, with great expectations. But the few buyers that come don't make an offer. The seller waits. The showings dwindle. The seller drops the price. No offers, few showings. There is a For Sale sign out front for all the neighbors to see, and the home sits on the market without an offer, and few prospective buyers are coming to see it. How eager is that seller to receive an offer at this point? You may be able to pick up a higher value home just by being the first buyer to make an offer.

Unfortunately for the seller, if the home had been priced right from the beginning, it would almost certainly have sold sooner and fetched more.

Roommates

As a final thought in making your first home purchase affordable, consider having a roommate for your first year or two to help with expenses. Any rent you charge will go toward your mortgage payment, increasing your equity. And speak to your lender. It may be that your lender will consider a signed rental agreement when calculating your debt-to-income ratio, enabling you to qualify more easily. If you do decide to take on a roommate, even if it's a good friend, be certain to have an attorney draw up a lease agreement and screen anyone you don't know well carefully. This will protect both you and the tenant; you'll need the lease anyway to prove the anticipated income to the lender.

The roommate option is a form of "house hacking" recommended by savvy investor sites such as Bigger Pockets.

Home Work

 Determine the type of home you're looking for and the general location, but plan to be flexible.

11: KNOW YOUR MARKET; SELECT AN AGENT

A house is one of the largest purchases you'll ever make. It's important for you to know and understand your market. Scour local listings for homes in the price range you identified in Chapter 8. Use Zillow, the multiple listing service for your area, Redfin, Realtor.com. Even Craigslist. Attend open houses. Understand your negotiating position. If homes are selling quickly with multiple offers, you're in a seller's market, with all the negotiating power in the seller's hands. When you find yourself in a seller's market, you need to shop at a *lower price point* than the one you can afford. This will give you an advantage over other prospective buyers because you'll be able to offer above full price.

Once you have a good feel for the market, and not before, find the right real estate agent to represent you. Look for someone who's active in the market you're looking in. Before you start scouting for an agent though, let me clear up some misconceptions a lot of people have about real estate licensees.

How Buyer Agents Work

Licensees work strictly on commission. This means that they don't get paid unless and until they place you in a home and that home closes. While it's fine to "shop" for an agent before you commit, please don't end up working with more than one licensee at a time. Loyalty to one agent of your choosing will be rewarded with a higher level of service to you.

Along these lines, you might consider signing a buyer broker agreement. I no longer work with buyers without such an agreement in place. Early in my career I showed a woman 40 houses, several of which she asked to see multiple times so she could get the approval of her prospective roommates. Then she ghosted me. I tried to reach her several times and finally she confessed that she'd ended up buying a house using a licensee from her church. Lesson learned.

The benefit to signing on with one agent exclusively (during, for instance, a three-month period) is that you will receive the highest level of service from that agent. Buyer brokerage agreements may be structured either as a loyalty pledge (you will only use me to write the offer) or they may make you responsible for the buyer agent's compensation. I would not recommend you sign an agreement that puts you on the hook for commission. Commission is traditionally paid by the seller and then split between the buyer's broker and seller's broker.

If you're comfortable that this agent will work hard for you during this period, then signing a buyer broker agreement will create a higher level of loyalty. It has another benefit: The agent will be able to help you find the right house and not the house that's being shown that moment. If the agent feels you're possibly going to write an offer using another buyer agent, there will be incentive to get you committed to a house—any house— while on that agent's watch.

If you do sign exclusive buyer representation, be clear about this when touring open houses or talking to seller's agents or other agents. *"I'm represented by _____."* Ask your agent for several business cards you can hand to the listing agents at any open houses you may end up attending solo.

Again, buyers generally do NOT pay a real estate licensee's commission. This is paid by the seller to the listing agent, and the listing agent's firm pays the buyer agent's firm. Because you won't be paying an agent out of pocket, there's absolutely no reason for you to try to do this on your own. A good buyer's agent will know the market far better than you can learn in a few weeks of research.

Selecting a Buyer Agent

Do similar research you did when looking for a lender. This time, you can start by asking the lender for a referral (assuming you've selected a lender with experience working with first-time homebuyers). Otherwise:

If you know someone who just purchased a home, you might ask them for a referral. This option is best if they are also first-time home buyers. If they don't RAVE about their agent, move on.

Enter the following in Google search field:

[real estate agent] [first-time home buyer] [city/state]

Contact several large brokerages in your town and ask the receptionist who in their office has deep experience working with first-time home buyers. Receptionists are great sources of information.

Tip: Make sure you're talking to the front desk, and not a licensee who is doing floor-call duty or you may be given the licensee's own name.

Attend first time home buyer programs in your area to see if there's a real estate professional there you can get to know.

Check the web sites of real estate firms in your area and review the bios of the licensees. Look for one who specializes in first time home buyers.

Note: You should not select the *listing agent* (the seller's agent) of the home you intend to purchase as your agent. While some states allow an agent to represent both the buyer and seller (this is called dual agency), it's not in your best interest. A dual agent has divided interests and you want full representation.

Interviewing Buyer Agents

Here are a few questions you may want to ask buyer agents:

How long have you been in real estate?

What is your knowledge of the local market?

What portion of your practice is working with first-time homebuyers?

What is the average price range you work in?

What has been your experience with X program [the financing program you've selected]?

I'm looking in [$X] price range. What is your experience with transactions in this price range?

What is your preferred method of communication? How soon can you get back to me if I have a question?

Let's say I find a property online that we want to see. How much notice do you need to get me in for a showing?

What if you're unavailable? Do you have a partner you work with who can pinch hit for you? (In a tight market, this is crucial.)

Note: The licensee should give you a copy of an agency disclosure. The agency disclosure is a consumer pamphlet that tells you your rights and the agent's duties when representing you. It will also explain your representation options, and what services you can expect with each. The disclosure doesn't *create* an agency relationship; it merely informs you about what's possible. Be sure to read this and ask any questions you have.

I've Found My Agent! Now What?

Once you've found the lucky agent, be very specific about your timing, your criteria, your deal killers, and your must-haves. Ask to be set up for automatic email feeds within your price range. Agents may "bracket" your price range to be helpful. Unless it's a buyer's market (where homes are selling below list price), this is not helpful. Ask not to receive listings above your price range.

Also ask the agent:

What happens if I find a For Sale by Owner property on my own?

I want to live in the X neighborhood because of [list your desired characteristics]. Are there other neighborhoods I should consider that are similar?

Ask to review important forms (such as the purchase agreement) before you're required to sign them. You don't want the first time you read this document to be when you're excitedly writing your first offer.

Home Work

 Select an agent; begin to familiarize yourself with the market by reviewing listings in your price range.

12: GET TO KNOW
THE PURCHASE AGREEMENT

As we've discussed, you don't want the time you're excitedly writing an offer to be the first time you read the purchase agreement. Obtain a copy of one and review it now and make sure you understand its terms. Much of it will be boilerplate (legalese that's always the same, but read that anyway) but there will also be blanks to complete that are specific to your transaction. Your agent will help you determine how to complete these blanks. Study the legalese now and understand how the blanks are completed so you know the items you need to consider when making an offer.

A Purchase Agreement is a Binding Contract

The most important thing for you to understand about the purchase agreement is that once it has been agreed to and signed by both parties, it becomes a binding contract. And only those items committed in writing to the purchase agreement are binding. Therefore, don't enter into a purchase agreement lightly, and don't rely on oral commitments; get all terms in writing.

Because it's binding, it's important for you to thoroughly read the purchase agreement before the heat of an offer. Following are some blanks your agent will help you complete when the time is right:

- **Who the parties are (buyer and seller)** and who represents whom: Your agent represents you as the buyer's agent. The seller's agent represents the seller as the seller's agent. Never share any confidential information with the seller's agent. The seller's agent has a duty to then share it with the seller!
- **The address and legal description** of the property
- **How the property will be conveyed** (deed, contract)
- **Your offer price.** This will be dependent on the house's list price, your ability to pay, and the market value of the home (which your agent will help you determine).
- **How much you intend to finance** and what type of financing you'll be using.
- **The amount of earnest money** you will put down, where it will be deposited, and within how many days

it will be deposited.

- **When you intend to close.** This will be a date usually 30-60 days from the date the offer is accepted. Confirm your lender's ability to meet this deadline.

- **Which entity is conducting the closing** (attorney, title company, brokerage office)

- **When you will take possession of the property** (usually on the day of closing, but everything is negotiable)

- **The deadline by which the seller must respond to** your offer

- **What personal items are being conveyed** with the house (e.g., freestanding refrigerator, washer and dryer)

- **What type of inspections** you're reserving the right to have done and by when

- **What contingencies you're reserving,** for instance:

   o The inspection contingency gives you a specified number of days to inspect the property (using a professional inspector) for defects and negotiate any repairs with the seller. You specify how long this continency remains in place. If you're unable to come to an agreement during this time with the seller, you can terminate and get a refund of your earnest money deposited. Why not ask for a long time, then? Sellers won't want to leave the home off the market while you conduct inspections for an inordinate amount of time. Ask your agent what's customary in your area (for instance, 10 business days).

o **The finance contingency** specifies that if you're unable to obtain financing after making a good faith effort to do so, you can terminate and get a refund of your earnest money deposited. You've been pre-approved, so you can imagine the seller will have some questions if you invoke this contingency.

o **The appraisal contingency** states that if the property doesn't appraise for the agreed upon sales price, you can terminate and get a refund of your earnest money deposited. Generally, when this occurs (and it's rare) the parties end up negotiating a reduction in the sales price or the buyer (you in this case) agrees to put more money down, or some combination of the two.

Time is of the Essence

As you can see, there are plenty of contingencies built in for the buyer to protect your earnest money. What the purchase agreement doesn't protect you from are your own missed deadlines (including the ability to close by the deadline specified), your failure to act in good faith, or any other breach of the contract.

There's a phrase in real estate, "time is of the essence." It means both parties agree not to unduly delay the progression toward closing. Honor your deadlines. If you don't, you can be found to have breached the contract, putting your earnest money at risk. If you find you are going to miss a deadline, try to negotiate an extension (your agent can prepare an addendum extending the deadline, but the seller isn't obligated to sign it and may decide to hold you to the original terms). Therefore, don't delay unnecessarily.

I've only ever had one instance where the other party delayed and continued to miss deadlines and it was when I represented the buyer for an estate property (a property where the owner had died). The heirs of the former owner were represented by a law firm and the law firm continually missed deadlines, necessitating my client to have to reschedule her movers, extend her lease, and incur other inconveniences and expenses. My client's only recourse (when breach after breach of our agreement occurred) was to terminate and get her earnest money back. But she didn't want to terminate, so we hung in there, at the mercy of the law firm which was certainly racking up legal fees during all the delays. Consider this fair warning: If the other party is a team of attorneys, prepare for all the built-in conventions of the transactional process to be thrown out the window. Law firms march to the beat of their own billable hour.

Home Work

Obtain a copy of the purchase agreement and read through it thoroughly. Imagine filling in the blanks for a fictitious offer, even though your agent will do this for you when it's time. Familiarizing yourself with this document will help bring down your anxiety level when you're making an offer for real.

13: TIME TO FIND A HOUSE!

Now comes the fun part! Armed with your must-haves and deal killers for your *just right* home, and being fully aware of your market, and having your real estate agent selected, it's time to begin shopping in your *just right* price range.

How's the Market?

Is it a seller's market? Shop in a price range 5-10% below where you qualify.

Is it a balanced market? Shop in your comfortable price range.

Is it a buyer's market? Shop in a price range just slightly above your comfortable price range. You may be able to negotiate down. But check with your agent: On average, how are homes that meet your criteria selling as compared to their list price? If they're selling at 97% of list price, you can shop slightly above your price, knowing you may be able to get your *just right* home for less.

Create a Plan

As mentioned, ask your agent to sign you up for a regular listing feed meeting your criteria. The multiple listing service has filters for price, location, type of home, size, and age. Consider house hunting a part-time job and dedicate specific times of day or days of the week to it. On the weekend, attend open houses:

- In your favorite areas in any price range
- In multiple areas in your price range

This will give you an idea of what's available.

Drive through your favorite neighborhoods and look for new For Sale signs.

For Sale By Owners

In addition to the multiple listing service, drive-throughs of your favorite neighborhoods, and scouring REO sites, don't ignore For Sale by Owner sellers (called FSBOs and pronounced fizz-bos). These often appear in Craigslist and on For Sale by Owner sites. You may want to have your agent approach the seller first. He or she can ask whether the seller offers "courtesy to brokers," which means the seller is willing to pay a buyer agent commission to the agent who brings in the buyer. If the seller does not offer courtesy to brokers, this is a situation you'll need to discuss with your agent. In fact, this should have been discussed during the interview process with your agent, because a licensee has no duty to represent you when there will be no compensation. If the seller does offer courtesy to brokers, your agent will make it clear that the agent represents you and not the seller.

One caveat in working with FSBOs: often they've opted not to be represented because they have an inflated idea of what their home is worth, and no listing agent will agree to take the listing at that price. If you decide to present an offer to an unrepresented seller who does not offer courtesy to brokers, you may need to hire an attorney to protect your interests.

Scheduling Showings; Confidentiality

Unless there is an open house, your agent will need to arrange showings for any properties you want to see. When touring a home, be aware that nanny cams may be in use. Don't say anything that would either upset a seller or give the seller an advantage over you in negotiations should you decide to make an offer. That discussion should take place outside of the home.

How to Keep it All Straight When Touring Houses

It will happen: You'll see more than three houses and suddenly they all start running together. I have a couple of tricks to keep that from happening:

Nicknames: Give each house worth considering a nickname. "The Dairy Queen House" was a nickname some of my clients used because it was on the way to their favorite drive-through. "The Grandma House" is one another client of mine used because the home reminded her of her grandmother's house.

Checklist: I provide my clients with a checklist and rating form which I attach to the multiple listing service posting (which will have the address, the square footage, number of bedrooms, and number of bathrooms). What usually ends up happening, though is that they often get so animated during the house touring process that these rarely get filled out in completion. But having anything written down can help recall. If you end up creating your own checklist, include your deal killers and must-haves. And be prepared for these not to matter as much as you think they did when you eventually find your *just right* home.

House Hunt Checklist

	Ranking: 1=poor, 4=excellent)			
Amenity	1	2	3	4
Location				
Exterior				
Condition				
Age				
Size				
Layout				
Living room				
Kitchen				
Dining				
Family				
Bedrooms				
Bathrooms				
Walls/Trim				
Move-in Ready?				
Windows/light				
Storage				
Basement				
Garage				

Keep Resale in Mind

When house shopping, don't get so blinded by a feature you love that you overlook a feature that would turn most buyers off and that can never be made right.

I once showed a home to a blended family with five young children. The home was laid out like a rabbit warren. The ceilings were low, the hallways narrow, and unpermitted work was obvious at every corner. But because it had been freshly painted and fit their family better than their current cramped conditions, the couple was determined to have this house.

To compound the issue, this was in 2006 when *stated income, no documentation* financing was available. Had the financing standards been stricter, it's unlikely the couple would have qualified for a loan. Learning they could purchase their own home was a thrilling proposition to them. They bought the house, taking on a mortgage they couldn't really afford, and a year later, when the market took a nose dive, he was transferred out of town for work. They wanted to sell the house and called me to prepare a competitive market analysis. I had to tell them that the market value was lower than what they paid for their home.

Because they had bought it at an inflated value and because its layout wasn't to most people's liking, their chances of a sale were minimal. They ended up renting it out at less than their mortgage payment and moving into a tiny rental in their new town.

I share this as a cautionary tale. While *you* know what you want in a house, consider whether it will appeal to the broader market. A one-bedroom, one-bathroom condo has broad appeal. A one-bedroom, one-bathroom 2,000 square foot home does not. Nor does a five-bedroom, 1,400 square foot home.

This leads to another topic—emotional appeal. The reason "buyers are liars" is because they often fall in love with a property for reasons that never made it to their must-have list and may even contain features they swore were deal killers. This happens because buying a home isn't the same as buying any other asset. We get emotionally involved. We can usually remain coolly objective when we fund our 401(k) or invest in the stock market. But when shopping for a home, our imagination and emotions get added to the mix and we think about what it will be like looking out the kitchen window with a cup of coffee in our hand, or how fun it will be tossing laundry down the chute in the hall closet or how our friends will enjoy the wine parties we host on the deck in the summer. And that's all good. I hope you do feel emotionally invested in the place you're going to call home. But don't let emotions rule what also needs to be a practical decision.

This goes two ways. Don't let a minor feature that turns you off about a home (*ugh, who puts red shag carpeting in their dining room?*) keep you from purchasing what could in fact be your *just right* home with a little makeover.

Ask your agent's opinion. Your agent should be able to give you an idea of whether a neighborhood is undergoing revitalization, whether a floor plan has broad appeal, and cost approximations (and return on investment) for renovations and cosmetic improvements.

You'll Likely Find Your House First

Don't expect your agent to find your *just right* house for you. Your agent will be vested in finding you a home, certainly, but no one can compete with the level of interest you have in finding your home. In nearly 20 years as a broker, I can count on one hand the times it was me who found my buyers a home. I've come to accept that it's not because I'm a lousy agent; my buyers just know what they're looking for (and they often change their minds about what that is). In any case, my real value comes later in the transaction: negotiation and follow-through to closing.

Home Work

Determine whether you're in a seller's, buyer's, or balanced market. Establish a house hunting schedule to include showings, online research, and drive-throughs of your favorite neighborhood.

14: MAKE AND NEGOTIATE AN OFFER

Congratulations! You've found your *just right* home and you're ready to make an offer. This is where your agent earns his or her stripes. All that preliminary work: establishing your criteria, scheduling showings, touring properties, was just a prelude to how agents really earn our fees. This is where it gets exciting for a real estate professional, and probably a little nerve-wracking for you.

Now that you've identified a home, before you make an offer, your agent should prepare a comparative market analysis (CMA) to help you determine whether the home is appropriately priced and what a fair offering price would be.

Is it overpriced? Underpriced? Are there other interested parties? These are important considerations when determining an offering price. Hopefully, you're within your affordability comfort zone. If so, your agent may suggest that you offer full price. However, if it's a buyer's market or the home has been on the market a while without an offer (and the home didn't just experience a price drop) you may not need to offer full price.

If all lights are green (home is priced fairly and the market is either balanced or favors sellers somewhat), go ahead and make a full price offer. If it's slightly overpriced, you may want to offer slightly less than the list price.

Ways to sweeten a less than full price offer include:

- **Offer to close sooner.** Make sure your lender can meet whatever deadline you set.

- **Allow the seller a grace period to vacate.** That means the seller can remain in the home for a few days after closing. This is helpful for some sellers who need their funds from the sale to pay their moving expenses.

- **Shorten the usual inspection period.** Most purchase agreements will have a default inspection period (for instance, 10 business days). It's a time when the seller loses 8 pounds of sweat because the home is now off the market (it goes sale pending when the seller accepts your offer) and the seller is losing precious marketing time waiting to find out if the deal is really going to happen.

- Offer to buy the home as-is. Don't worry. You'll still do an inspection, and you can pull out if the inspection turns up a repair you can't live with. Chances are, though, the seller would rather negotiate that repair with you than have you walk away, so "as-is" just notifies the seller you're not going to be unreasonable.

Asking the Seller to Pay Your Closing Costs

There is one instance where you may want to pay more than list price, and not just because the market is hot or you're up against other buyers. You may want to pay more than list price so you can ask the seller to cover your closing costs. We discussed this earlier, but here's another example:

Avery makes an offer on 4550 Randall Street. The house is listed at $185,000, but Avery writes his offer for $190,000 and includes a clause in the purchase agreement:

"Seller to pay $5,000 toward buyer's closing costs."

Does the seller mind? No, because the net to the seller is essentially the same. It's not *quite* the same because the seller pays commission on the sales price and the sales price is now inflated by $5,000. But most sellers wouldn't mind or frankly notice this discrepancy and it's up to the seller's agent to point this out.

The other issue here, which I believe most seller's agents will (or at least should point out) is, what happens if the property doesn't appraise at $190,000? If the property appraises at only $185,000, the seller likely won't want to drop the price another $5,000 since he just gave up $5,000 in closing costs. Most properties appraise at value but adding closing costs to the sales price carries risks that the seller should be made aware of.

What if the Offer Is Rejected?

In a perfect world, the seller will accept your offer and all its terms at face value. How often does this happen? Maybe 50% of the time in a balanced market. In a buyer's market, more often. In a seller's market, rarely. In a seller's market, there may be many competing offers, and the highest offer with the best terms will almost certainly win.

If the seller likes your offer enough to work with you, but there's something about your offer the seller would like to change, the seller's only option is to counter your offer. Make no mistake: a counteroffer kills the original offer. It says, *"No, I don't agree to this. But will you agree to THIS?"* The counteroffer spells new terms the seller *would* agree to. Usually only one or two items are changed in the original offer and the counter offer will specify only those items that are changing. For instance,

I've underlined the two items that the following counteroffer attempts to change:

"Sales price to be <u>$215,000</u>. Closing date to be <u>March 23</u>, 20XX. All other terms and conditions to remain the same."

In the above instance, the seller has countered the sales price and the closing date. All the other terms from the original offer were retained.

What happens if you don't like the seller's counteroffer? You can counter the counteroffer. Then the seller can counter your countered counteroffer and so on ... Usually by the sixth round, everyone's heads are spinning, but it rarely goes that far.

The important takeaway is that a counteroffer kills the original offer, so only counter on important items. Let's take one more example to make this point clear.

1. You make an offer on the seller's home for $205,000.

2. The seller counters at $208,000.

3. You counter at $206,500.

4. The seller rejects your counter.

Can you now go back to the seller and say, *"Just kidding, we'll take it for $208,000"?* Not without creating new paperwork and obtaining signatures from both parties. Deal #1 died when the seller countered with #2. Deal #2 died when you countered at #3. Dead is dead. So be careful what you counter and make sure it's worth losing the deal over.

In negotiation, both parties will give up something. Strive for a win-win, stay firm on what matters to you, but keep your eye on the prize.

Other Paperwork Beyond the Purchase Agreement

Counteroffers may be prepared on specifically labeled counteroffer forms or on addenda amending the terms of the agreement. Other addenda and documents that will be part of the offer process are:

- **Buyer preapproval letter** (this letter, which you obtain from your lender, should be provided with your offer)
- **Seller disclosures:** This is a checklist of everything the seller knows regarding the condition of the property (in most states, this must be provided to the buyer soon after the offer is accepted or at the time of making the offer and the buyer then has a specified number of days to review the disclosures and either approve or unconditionally disapprove and terminate the offer)
- **Lead-based paint disclosure:** This is required for properties built prior to 1978 when lead was phased out

of paint manufacturing. The buyer must also receive a copy of an EPA pamphlet titled Protect Your Family from Lead in the Home, warning buyers about the dangers of lead poisoning. Buyers are also given time in the purchase agreement to test the home for lead, but I've never seen a buyer do this. If the home was built prior to 1978 there is lead in the paint, it's likely been painted over many times, and unless someone is chewing on painted surfaces (which young children may do!) most people won't bother testing.

- Surveys, where required
- Pest inspection reports, where required

Buyer Responsibilities with an Accepted Offer

Once your offer is accepted, you have a clock ticking against all deadlines in the purchase agreement. You must:

- Open escrow (your agent will provide copies of the completed purchase agreement to the closing officer).
- Deposit earnest money at the location and by the deadline stipulated.
- Make a loan application with your preferred lender. Your lender will need a copy of the completed purchase agreement and will provide you with a copy of the Loan

Estimate, within three days. This is a close approximation of your closing costs.

- **Review and sign the disclosures**; your agent will provide a copy to the seller's agent.
- **Schedule inspections** (your agent will help you do this; you should plan to attend).

Home Work

 If this is just a dry run (no offer yet), ask your agent for copies of the seller disclosure form so you can see what one looks like. If this is the real thing, your agent will get you the real one.

Negotiation Tip:

When negotiating repairs (next chapter) consider including a throw-away item. Ask for everything you want (within reason) but include one item that isn't really that important to you. When the seller looks over your requests, this item should stand out as maybe asking for "too much." This gives you a psychological advantage. If the seller says "no" to that item, it will be harder for the seller to say "no" to the items that mean more to you. Sellers don't want to appear unreasonable.

15: THE HOME INSPECTION

A key first step as soon as you have an accepted offer (beyond depositing the earnest money as agreed) is to review seller disclosures (if you haven't already) and then schedule a home inspection.

Your agent likely has a short list of recommended inspectors you can select from or you're welcome to find one on your own. Can you skip the home inspection? Not on my watch. In fact, I've never had a client (or even a buyer when I was representing the seller) waive a home inspection. Not even for new construction (and I'll explain why that is in a moment).

The only time I've seen the inspection contingency waived was during a sizzling hot seller's market in Seattle. I was visiting some friends and we toured an open house where the listing agent had a desk set up at the entrance to the home. She was taking names of open house visitors and telling us the rules.

136

"The seller is not accepting any offers containing inspection contingencies."

She explained to us that, because very few homes were available, sellers were now requiring buyers to perform preemptive inspections before making their offers, allowing buyers to then waive the inspection contingency when they did make their offers. All buyers were given a five-day window in which to conduct their inspections. So prospective buyers each shelled out several hundred dollars for a home inspection, not knowing whether their offer would even be accepted.

Why Inspections Are Required

As mentioned, in most states, the seller will provide the buyer with a signed disclosure form detailing any defects known to the seller about the property so the buyer can decide whether to move forward with the transaction. Let's say the seller provided you with this form, you've thoroughly reviewed it, and there were no red flags. Given this, what's the point of the inspection? Two points actually:

- Not every seller is honest.
- The seller doesn't know everything.

How often do sellers slither around in their crawl space, climb on their roofs, or take a flashlight to the rafters in the attic looking for signs of moisture? What about checking every accessible pipe in the house for leaks and every ground fault circuit interrupter outlet to ensure they're grounded? A good home inspector covers every accessible area of the house like a defect-seeking missile, after which he or she will prepare a report with photos and maintenance or repair suggestions. The inspector may also recommend that the buyer schedule follow-up visits with specialized inspectors for the roof and HVAC system. The home inspection itself may cost a few hundred dollars ($350-$600 depending on the size of the house and what the market will bear).

Additional inspections that may be required are:

- Radon testing ($125 or so)
- Mold spore testing (varies)
- Roof inspection (varies)
- HVAC inspection (varies)
- Electrical inspection (varies)
- Sewer scope ($125 or so)
- Underground oil tank search and soil sample ($150 or so)
- Pest inspection ($150 or so)

New Construction

New construction properties also need inspections, even though the city inspector will be out there regularly to permit the work while the home is being built.

Why inspect what's brand new? Things happen. What if the sewer line to the street separates at a joint when a subcontractor rolls over it with heavy equipment?

In the Portland, Oregon, area where I practice, the biggest inspection items (those that cause the most issues for buyers and sellers are):

Roofs (age, defects, improper installing, leaks) – if an inspector deems that there is less than five years' life left on a roof, it will be flagged, and it may cause issues with the appraisal and buyer financing. A roof *repair* may not cost much, maybe a few hundred dollars, but a roof replacement can cost $10,000 or more.

Underground oil tanks – These used to be common in some areas and if they weren't properly decommissioned or are still in use and are leaking, any environmental damage that occurs is on the owner to clean up. If it's not discovered during the inspection, then the buyer is the owner, and it will become the buyer's responsibility to clean up and decommission the tank when contamination is discovered. This can cost $3,000-

$5,000 or more depending on the extent of the contaminated soil.

Sewer lines – not only do these break and clog, but roots can intrude on them, they can become separated, and sometimes they are "party lined" with the neighbors. The city used to allow party lines where only one line went to the street, the other tied in to the neighbor's line. If an inspection occurs and one line needs to be replaced, both parties must separate their lines and create new lines to the street. Explain that to your neighbors when you're trying to close on your house. *"Hey, Bob, can you please put in a new sewer line so I can get my work permitted and close on my house? It will only cost you a few thousand dollars."*

Radon – Radon is an odorless, colorless gas that occurs in the soil when uranium breaks down. When it enters our breathing space in concentrated quantities it can cause severe health issues. Radon is the leading cause of lung cancer in non-smokers. And most people don't know they have it or that they should test for it. Radon kits are easy to get at any hardware store. The type I've used has two canisters you open for a few days, then cap, label and send to a lab. The kit is less than $15 and the lab fee is $40. And if high levels are found, radon mitigation is a relatively inexpensive proposition and can bring radon down to safer levels within a day or two. So, don't let a high level scare you off, just make sure a mitigation system is installed.

Negotiating Repairs

When the home inspection occurs, plan to be there. The seller should *not* be there. You can follow the inspector around and pick up maintenance tips for the house that may not make it into the report. You probably don't want to follow the inspector on the roof or under the house, and maybe stay out of the unfinished attic, but otherwise, you should stick close. At the end, the inspector will either share the report with you right then or send it to you by email within a day.

Expect there to be issues. There are *always* issues but decide what's worth asking the seller to address. If an issue is not a structural or a health concern or a big-ticket item, you should probably just accept it as part of owning a home. (This isn't the case with new construction, however, where even cosmetic items can be added to a "punch list" and the builder will usually be happy to fix these).

Let's say though that it's something that doesn't need to be addressed right away but will cost you money sooner than you'd planned. For instance, the electric water heater is 18 years old. With a lifetime expectancy of 10-15 years, you're going to need a new water heater soon. Do you budget for it or ask the seller for a credit at closing? That probably depends on a couple of things: How amenable do you think the seller will be to a credit, and how much have you already asked for in credits? Remember that some programs limit the amount of credit a seller can give you. Discuss this with your agent and make the call.

Other issues that may occur during inspections are:

- Mold is found
- Unpermitted work is discovered
- A portion of the home was constructed or remodeled with recalled materials
- Evidence of pest or rodent intrusion
- Failed thermal seals in windows
- Moisture intrusion
- Foundation cracks/settling
- Slow drains in tubs, sinks
- Plumbing leaks
- Siding issues (moisture penetration)
- Shrubbery growing too close to the house
- Drainage issues in the yard
- Water in the crawl space
- Missing smoke alarms and carbon monoxide detectors

It's good for you to see what can crop up so you won't be thrown off when the inspector calls out some of these issues during your inspection. It's the inspector's job to point out any defects. It's your job to decide what's important enough to ask for and whether not getting what you ask for is important enough to lose the house over.

Home Work

Ask your agent what type of issues generally come up during home inspections in your area. And if you've not done so yet, you may want to have the radon tested in your current property. What you don't know can hurt you!

16: ORDER THE APPRAISAL

Once the inspection appears to have gone well or you've at least come to terms with the seller on items that must be addressed, it's time to order the appraisal.

Ask your lender how long it takes to schedule an appraiser in your market. Usually, it's just a couple of weeks. Therefore, I always recommend that you complete your inspections and any repair negotiation *before* you order the appraisal. Why? If the deal is going to fall apart over the inspection, you don't want to also be out the cost of the appraisal (which will cost just as much or more than the home inspection). So, wait on the appraisal until the inspection hurdle is cleared if you possibly can. Usually this works out.

Your lender will order your appraisal. This is a good time to mention that throughout this process your lender has likely been asking you for paperwork and documentation and at some point, you're going to think you've already given your lender everything and your lender is going to come back and ask for more. Probably more than a few times.

The underwriter, the person who is deciding whether your lender should lend you the money, wants you to get the loan, but also wants to make sure her employer (the lender) doesn't lose by financing your loan. When the underwriter asks you for something, track it down and provide it quickly. She's on your side, even if she is the single biggest pain in your neck you have ever experienced and why didn't she just ask you for that last time she called?!

Keep the underwriter happy while you're taking care of the inspection and repair negotiations and all will be well with your loan.

Unless ...

Unless the appraisal report comes in and the house doesn't appraise at the agreed upon sales price.

In that case you and the seller have three options:

- You can renegotiate the sales price.
- You can pony up some cash to make up the difference between appraised value and sales price (or the seller can meet you half way).
- You can terminate the deal and get your earnest money

back, but you're now out nearly a grand between the inspection and the appraisal.

The good news? That probably won't happen. Appraisers provide an estimate of value at a given moment in time. To arrive at this estimate of value, they use several complicated formulas and plug in a slew of numbers following the Uniform Standards of Professional Appraisal Practice (USPAP) and … it's still their best guess. Appraisals nearly always come in at exactly the agreed upon sales price, and no one is surprised.

On one hand, that sounds like a rip off. *What are we paying them for, anyway?*

On the other hand, it makes sense. In a real estate transaction, we have a willing buyer (that's you) and a willing seller in a free market agreeing on a price. Therefore, that price *is* the best estimate of market value at that moment in time. But the lender still must do due diligence and order the appraisal.

So, don't worry too much about whether the property will appraise. It nearly always does.

Home Work

 After the appraisal comes in, the only real hurdle left to clear is financing. Keep your underwriter happy and you're almost home free!

17: PREPARE TO CLOSE

Congratulations! You found a home, your offer has been accepted, and you've made it past the inspection and appraisal hurdles. That's it right? *Not quite.*

There's still financing to get through. Let's talk about how underwriting works (besides all those calls you've been getting).

How Underwriting Works

When an underwriter reviews your file, she will verify your income, assets, debt, and the property's details before your loan will receive final approval. The underwriter will continue to ask you for documents and answers to questions throughout the underwriting process, right up until just a few days before your loan is approved.

In doing this, the underwriter is trying to determine how much of a risk your lender will take on if it decides to grant you a loan. In a way, the underwriter is protecting both you and the bank, even if it may sometimes feel as though this is not so. The underwriter doesn't want the bank to lose money lending to you and doesn't want you getting in over your head on a mortgage you can't afford.

The underwriter will look at your credit score, pull your credit report, and ask you for explanations for any late payments or overuse of credit, or for other anomalies. You'll be asked to prove your income and verify that your employment situation is steady. The underwriter will evaluate your DTI ratio and verify your down payment and savings.

Underwriting can take a few to several weeks. You have very little control over the timing, but you can help speed the process by providing the required documentation and explanations when asked. Be completely honest about your financial situation and be prepared to explain past mistakes. You may be required to provide an explanatory letter, for instance, for a late payment. This is as simple as a single-page typewritten letter that you sign and date that may read something like this:

[Date]

To whom it may concern. In April of 20XX, I fell ill and missed three weeks of work. At that time, I missed one payment on my Bank of America VISA ending in 4456. I quickly caught up on my payments the following month.

Signed, [Your signature]

When your loan is "in underwriting," the underwriter will evaluate your finances and past credit decisions, plus the property, looking at:

- Income: W-2s, bank statements, and pay stubs will be required, or if you're self-employed, you'll need to provide profit and loss sheets, balance sheets, and your personal and business tax returns.

- Appraisal: After the appraiser determines an estimate of value for the property, the underwriter will compare this amount to the amount of your mortgage. If the home is worth much less than the mortgage, your underwriter may suspend your application. As said, this is a rare occurrence.

- Credit: The underwriter will evaluate your credit score. A good credit score shows that you pay back your debts and can also help you qualify for a lower interest rate. Your DTI will be calculated. Don't apply for any new credit while you're in underwriting. Any significant financial changes or spending can interrupt your underwriting process. Don't make big purchases that will decrease your funds.

Warning: Your credit score will be pulled again just prior to funding your loan. Don't think just because you've made it through underwriting that you can go put living room furniture on layaway (even if the store promises not to charge you any interest for 12 months, the debt will show up on your credit). *Don't do anything to impact your credit until after closing.*

At least three days prior to closing, you should receive a copy of your Closing Disclosure. This should look like the Loan Estimate your lender provided when you made your application. It will contain the exact amount you'll need to bring to closing, and all the closing costs to the penny. Let's discuss closing costs next.

How Closing Costs Work

Closing costs are the funds you'll need to bring to close on your new home. On the day you sign your final closing paperwork, you'll bring your photo I.D. and the exact amount of money required to close. A personal check won't work for this; it must be a cashier's check or wired funds. Before you wire anything, however, verify, verify, verify that you're wiring it to the right place. Don't ever accept a last-minute change in wiring instructions. Scammers have been known to scrape email addresses of people involved in real estate transactions and redirect funds into their own bank accounts. Once the money is gone, it's gone. Wire fraud has cost people many thousands of dollars.

Your closing costs will cover the fees and pre-paid items that are part of the cost of buying a home. Sellers have their own fees to pay, but let's concentrate on yours for now. You'll be required to pay:

- Lender fees, such as credit reports, loan origination fees, any points, appraisal, and underwriting fees
- Title and escrow fees, such as your portion of the title insurance, the title search fee, escrow deposits for reserves (taxes and insurance), and recording fees

And of course, your largest cost will be your down payment on your loan. Hopefully, you got help in the form of gifted funds, a grant, or down payment assistance. If not, great job saving up.

Some fees the seller pays will come down on the plus side of your equation at closing. These include any prorated taxes or homeowners association dues, and the seller will cover transfer taxes and recording fees and the seller's portion of the title insurance. The seller will also pay broker commissions for the seller's agent's office and your agent's office. And the seller will pay off any existing mortgage and/or home equity loans from the proceeds of the sale.

Prepaids and Prorates

Two terms you'll want to be familiar with regarding closing costs are prepaids and prorates.

Prepaids: A prepaid item is an item that you pay upfront at closing before it's due. These may include:

- A year's worth of homeowners insurance
- Prepaid property taxes (usually two months' worth must be paid upfront)
- Prepaid mortgage interest, which is based on the number of days between closing and the last day of the month, will be applied to your first mortgage payment. You can lower the amount of money you'll need to bring to closing by scheduling your closing date closer to month's end.

Prepaid funds are held by escrow in "reserve" (which is how they're often referred to).

Prorations: Prorations are calculations for expenses either prepaid by the seller, which must be reimbursed by you, or "enjoyed" by the seller before being paid for, in which case they must be credited to you. Prorations show up as credits and debits on your closing statement. They ensure that both parties pay their fair share of the costs associated with the home at the time each owns the home. Let's say, for instance, that the seller has paid that year's homeowners association dues in advance. But the sale is occurring at the end of February. Therefore, you must reimburse the seller for the association dues from March through the end of the year. This prorated amount will show up as a credit on the seller's closing statement and a debit on your closing statement.

How a Title Search Works

One of the closing costs you'll be required to pay is for a title search, and this ranges from $75 to $200. A title search ensures that the seller has the right to sell the property to you and there are no other claims on the title. Title searches may not turn up everything, though, so title companies will also issue title insurance (for a one-time fee) ensuring you against future claims on the title.

How Property Taxes Are Paid

Property taxes may be calculated differently depending on where you live. But usually, they're based on the value of your home and property. *Ad valorem* is the Latin term for this and simply means "according to value." But let's say you see the assessed value of your property and it's far less than what you paid. Are you paying too much? Probably not. Many states use lower assessment ratios when calculating tax assessments. In some cases, a state might only tax property based on 50% of its actual value.

Except for the reserves that you'll be required to place in escrow when you close, or 30 years from now when you pay your home off, you won't be paying property taxes separately. That's because most loans spread annual property taxes out throughout the year and are paid with your monthly mortgage payment (insurance is handled this way as well).

The Insurance Binder

Before you can close on your loan, your lender is going to require you to get a homeowners insurance policy and provide proof of that coverage. This is something you need to arrange in advance of signing your closing paperwork. Contact your insurance company and ask for a homeowners insurance policy and bring proof of coverage to closing. That proof comes in the form of an insurance binder, which is a document that serves as proof of insurance. It provides key information such as the amount of coverage, the type of property being insured, your deductible amount, what's covered, and the length of the policy (effective date and expiration).

Good News About Your Mortgage

"Good news about your mortgage" isn't a phrase you hear too often, right? Well, check this out: in contrast to your rent, which must be paid in advance, your mortgage payment is made in *arrears*. This means, depending on which part of the month in which you close, you may not have a mortgage payment due for nearly two months! That ought to make all those closing fees a little more manageable. And maybe you can even afford some furniture, after all. *After* closing.

Home Work

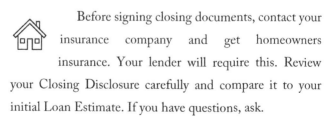 Before signing closing documents, contact your insurance company and get homeowners insurance. Your lender will require this. Review your Closing Disclosure carefully and compare it to your initial Loan Estimate. If you have questions, ask.

18: SIGNING DOCUMENTS; GETTING THE KEYS

Just before signing, unless you've agreed that the seller is retaining possession after closing, you'll want to do a final walk-through of your home. Make sure the home is in the order you expect it to be in:

- All requested repairs are made to your satisfaction.

- All seller possessions have been removed (or are in the process of being so).

- No items that were meant to be conveyed with the home have been removed.

- The home is in essentially the same condition as when you last saw it (no damage has occurred).

Basically, you're ensuring there won't be any surprises. If there are items of concern, address these before you sign the final paperwork. Getting sellers to address them after they have their money and have moved on may prove difficult.

Setting Up Your Utilities

You'll want to get your utilities ready to go a couple of weeks before moving day so that you're not trying to settle in without heat, water, electricity or, worse—no Wi-Fi! Contact your local utility providers and notify them of the upcoming change in ownership and the closing date. And don't forget to cancel the utilities and services on that date from your current providers.

Utilities and services to contact include:

- Electricity
- Natural gas
- Water and sewer
- Cable and internet
- Garbage and recycling service

You should also notify the U.S. Post Office of your change of address. *Bonus! You'll then be placed on a promotional list and will receive a welcome packet with coupons and other offerings from stores and restaurants in the area.*

How Closing Occurs

After you sign your closing paperwork, all documents are

sent to your lender. "Funding" of your loan is when funds transfer from your lender to the seller's account. When that happens, the closing officer will give the parties the "all clear" and will state, *"We're funded and released to record."*

Released to record means that the property can officially be publicly recorded as having changed hands. Practically speaking, this may not occur for several days, but legally, the property is yours!

This happy day (official closing) will occur either the day of signing if you've signed early in the morning or later that day. *It should occur no later than the day of closing specified in your purchase agreement.* If closing is delayed beyond that date, both parties must sign an addendum amending the closing date.

How You Get Your Keys

Usually, your agent will hand you the keys to your new house after the "all clear" is received from the closing officer. Often the listing agent will deliver the keys to your agent or leave them in the lockbox for your agent to pick up and deliver to you. Unless you and the seller have negotiated otherwise, usually you'll be able to move in at 5 p.m. on closing day!

Before You Leave ...

How to Buy a House gives you the tools, resources, and knowledge to become a homeowner if that's what you want to do. You've learned how to speak the language of real estate transactions like a pro.

You now know that any roadblocks you thought were standing between you and homeownership—credit, a lack of down payment, income—can be overcome with a little home work on your part. In fact, you now know several programs that were designed specifically for your circumstances. You know how to find the right lender and the right agent to help make your ownership dreams a reality. And when you do find that *just right* home, you're ready for the negotiation phase, the home inspection, the appraisal, underwriting, and the closing process.

You're at the starting line, and you're ready. The rest is up to you. I wish you every success in finding your *just right* home, and I would love to hear from you when you do! Please let me know what you found most helpful by leaving a review. I'd love for you to share a photo of you in front of your new home!

~ Yvonne

Home Work

 What are you waiting for? Go get that house! (Happy hunting!)

ACKNOWLEDGMENTS

This book came into being because of so many wonderful clients it has been my privilege to serve throughout the years. They're the inspiration for much of what you've read here. Every time I've thought of leaving this crazy business, I'm reminded what a privilege it is to be able to make a positive difference in others' lives. Thank you.

I learned much about loan options from Vince Kingston of Guild Mortgage, a self-proclaimed first-time home buyer evangelist, and Shane Musselwhite, mortgage broker for Oregon First, who has helped several of my clients find financing to suit their needs. And I and my clients owe a world of gratitude to Susan Walker, Walker Inspections, the finest home inspector I know.

I also owe a debt of gratitude to my sister and favorite editor, Kathlene Whinnery, who made suggestions for the final draft of this book and left it much improved.

Thank you also to Audrey, Julianne, LaRita, Sahara, Sara, and Sue for your continued support and encouragement. Everyone needs a tribe, and I'm lucky to have found mine.

This book is dedicated to Max and Sam, my two favorite clients since the day they were born, and to Billie: Thank you. The way opened.

RESOURCES AND FURTHER READING

The 2007-2008 Financial Crisis in Review. (n.d.). Investopedia. Retrieved March 14, 2021, from https://www.investopedia.com/articles/economics/09/financial-crisis-review.asp

Asamoah, B. J. (2021, March 4). Do Landlords Have to Allow Emotional Support Animals? Know the Laws. Copyright (c)2004-2021 BiggerPockets, LLC. https://www.biggerpockets.com/blog/house-hackers-screen-tenants

Bungalow | Easy Coliving, Great Roommates, Flexible Leasing. (n.d.). Bungalow.Com. Retrieved March 14, 2021, from https://bungalow.com/articles/oregons-rent-control-law-explained

Crew, K. (2020, October 6). A Homeowner's Net Worth Is 40x Greater Than a Renter's. Keeping Current Matters. https://www.keepingcurrentmatters.com/2020/10/07/a-homeowners-net-worth-is-40x-greater-than-a-renters

Eligibility requirements for VA home loan programs. (n.d.). Veterans Affairs. Retrieved March 14, 2021, from https://www.va.gov/housing-assistance/home-loans/eligibility/

Home Possible Mortgages Overview - Freddie Mac. (n.d.). Freddie Mac. Retrieved March 14, 2021, from http://www.freddiemac.com/homepossible/index.html

HomeReady Mortgage | Fannie Mae. (n.d.). Fannie Mae. Retrieved March 14, 2021, from https://singlefamily.fanniemae.com/originating-underwriting/mortgage-products/homeready-mortgage

HUD Good Neighbor Next Door Program | HUD.gov / U.S. Department of Housing and Urban Development (HUD). (n.d.). HUD. Retrieved March 14, 2021, from https://www.hud.gov/program_offices/housing/sfh/reo/goodn/gnndabot

Schwartz, C. (2017, December 8). *Why Did the 30-Year Mortgage Rates Go as High as 18.45 Percent in Late 1981? |.* Loan Tik. https://www.loanatik.com/827-2/

Single Family Housing Guaranteed Loan Program | Rural Development. (n.d.). USDA. Retrieved March 14, 2021, from https://www.rd.usda.gov/programs-services/single-family-housing-guaranteed-loan-program

Solutions, R. (2020, November 25). *How Much House Can I Afford?* Daveramsey.Com. https://www.daveramsey.com/blog/how-much-house-can-i-afford

ABOUT THE AUTHOR

Yvonne Aileen has been a Portland, Oregon, real estate broker since 2003 and has been teaching real estate courses to licensees nationwide since 2011.

While in her undergraduate years, she received a real estate marketing newsletter that had been mass produced by a company in Ohio. Thinking it lacked local relevance, she decided to create her own newsletter, *Northwest Homefront*. She marketed *NWHF* to real estate licensees throughout the Portland area, achieving first-year revenues of more than $20,000. Years later, after obtaining her master's degree in writing, Ms. Aileen was making plans to create a regionally specific national newsletter when a friend suggested she obtain her real estate license to aid in that effort. This was right before the 2003 market boom.

Nearly two decades years later, she has yet to take that newsletter national.

Made in the USA
Monee, IL
09 April 2021